Beyond Inclusion

Beyond Inclusion

HOW TO RAISE ANTI-ABLEIST KIDS

CARRIE CHERNEY HAHN

CHICAGO

Published by Parenting Press
An imprint of Chicago Review Press Incorporated
814 North Franklin Street
Chicago, Illinois 60610
ISBN 978-0-914090-68-7

Library of Congress Control Number: 2024937142

Cover design: Jonathan Hahn
Typesetting: Nord Compo

Printed in the United States of America

CONTENTS

———

ACKNOWLEDGMENTS

——————

WE WERE ALL SITTING at the table one night for dinner: my husband; our older son, Pete (pseudonym chosen in honor of Peter Parker); our younger son, Dan (in honor of the inventor of BopIt, Dan Klitsner); and me. I told them I had something exciting to share, and then announced that I had been notified that a publishing company was going to make an offer for my book. I explained to the boys, "This means my book is going to happen." There were a few comments of celebration before I went on to say that I was very excited but also very nervous, because this was such a big deal and I still had so much to do. Dan got up from his seat right next to me, put his arms around me like he does when he is going in for hug, and whispered in my ear, "You can do this."

A little more than six years before this moment at the dinner table with my beautiful family of four, we were a family of three who saw the advocacy video of a beautiful boy in China and decided to pursue the goal of becoming his family. It is hard to explain what happened inside me the moment I first saw Dan in that video, but the word I always come back to is *urgency*. I felt an instant urgency to know

Dan. We were not even considering international adoption when I first saw him, and the entire idea seemed a little out of left field. We were interested in adoption but were days away from a licensing appointment to do foster care.

Without knowing me personally, you wouldn't know that I am a person who can decide to pass on an event downtown simply because the one-way streets and parking might be a little too overwhelming. Because that is the truth about me, I reflect with complete awe on the absolute calm I had about the daunting process of international adoption ahead of us. I had a little voice inside of me whispering *You can do this* from the beginning. Since that moment, a portion of my focus and attention has been on fulfilling the mission of making a safe place for Dan. It started with a home study and figuring out where we would obtain the services he would benefit from to support his access needs related to blindness and his therapeutic needs related to a very atypical first four and a half years of life. The mission has continued to include advocating for safety and inclusion in all the places where he spends time. I started to notice how common it was for people to be misinformed or underinformed about disability. This miseducation was a potential reason Dan lost his first family, and, combined with my mama bear instinct to make a safe place for him, it lit a fire inside me to learn and do as much as I can that might make a positive difference, for him and others. When we decided to adopt Dan, we were four years from knowing that Pete would be diagnosed with a learning disability. I had no idea that both of my children would be the greatest teachers I would ever know, and that they would lead me to at least one project—this book—that gives me passion and purpose. I am not the first to learn and grow through the pursuit of parenting. It is truly a gift. **To Pete and Dan: I am so incredibly thankful to be your mom. You bring so much joy to my life, and I am forever your biggest fan.**

I had tremendous teachers long before I became a mom, though. I started learning about disability when I was studying to become a speech-language pathologist (SLP). The academic learning in college and graduate school was important, but some of the "out of the textbook" stuff I learned has stuck with me as being of utmost importance. My graduate school advisor, Jane Wegner, was so strong in her convictions about self-determination and the importance of making sure that whatever we do with clients is meaningful to them. These gems of wisdom have made me a better SLP, as well as a better human. During a time when therapeutic techniques were veering toward erasing disability, she was steadfast in anti-ableism. *To Jane: Thank you for being a revolutionary.*

When I was in graduate school, I had the opportunity to participate in a grant project that paired me with a family whose members represent disability and neurodivergence. They welcomed me into their home and invited me to come to family functions. When I started providing respite care for their three precious children, who are all grown now, I knew very little about disability in general and even less about the ups and downs of living and parenting with disability. I was present for moments of joy and moments of devastation and everything in between. I will never be able to put into words the profound impact those two years had on me, and the words I will use to express my gratitude will fall short. *To Megan, Tom, Joshua, Nicky, and Mandy: Thank you for trusting me with your sacred experiences.*

In the fall of 2004, I started my career as an SLP at an agency in Wichita, Kansas, called Rainbows United Inc. This job set me up with a specialized experience that positioned me to be able to pursue professional interests going forward. I have always had the opportunity to do work that fuels me and, for the most part, have had bosses and supervisors who have poured into me and made me feel confident as a therapist. When I was preparing to leave Rainbows because we were moving to Texas, a beloved supervisor said to me, "I'll give you my blessing to leave under one condition: that I get a copy of your first book." I didn't have any books on my radar at that point. I laughed but felt my heart swell. To have people who believe in you is something special. *To Paco: Thank you for believing that I had big ideas and capabilities before I did.*

In my eighteen years as an SLP I have completed many hours of continuing education, but none have taught me as much as the clients I have had the honor of serving. Textbooks can teach you about the science of speech-sound production and language acquisition, interventions, and research. No textbook, though, can teach you about the ways individuality affects every aspect of what you do as a professional. Every child I have worked with has taught me something new and different that has helped me going forward, and I am so thankful for all the clients I have had the privilege of serving. So many are fierce self-advocates who have taught me to learn the beauty of meeting someone where they are rather than demanding that they join me where I am. They have introduced me to some beautiful places. There are too many to list, and I won't try because to forget a name would be personally inexcusable, but *To all my little teachers: Thank you for trusting me and for bringing me wisdom and joy.*

In these professional experiences with children, I have been witness to tenacious and unwavering parental advocacy. Long before I became the mom of disabled kids, I had the chance to learn from parents who were making safe spaces for their disabled and neurodivergent babes. Again, too many to name, but *To the parent advocates in my life: Your example helped me to be confident in the advocacy that I have needed to do for my boys. Thank you for loving your kids so well.*

Since I started saying words as an infant, there have been people in my life who have listened to my rantings about whatever I was passionate about at the moment. None of those closest to me are surprised that I have enough words to fill a book. In every moment when I was listened to and not dismissed or belittled, I gained little bits of self-assurance that nurtured an internal confidence suggesting I might have ideas worth listening to. *To Mom, Dad, Patrick, Bria, David, and the close friends I have always felt safe with: Thank you for never squashing the spirit of the girl who always has an abundance of words to share.*

This journey of diving into the experiences of disabled and neurodivergent people to become better educated has led me to the understanding that I, myself, am neurodivergent. Learning that I have ADHD has been profoundly impactful for me, and much of the research I have done for this book has been cathartic for me. *So, lastly: To the disabled and neurodivergent bloggers, social media influencers, content creators, and authors who have told the stories this book is built upon: Thank you for sharing your experiences so that others, like me, feel more comfortable stepping into our truth.*

My son says I can do this, so here I go.

INTRODUCTION

T HE SEED THAT WOULD GROW into this book probably sprouted back in
2004, when I finished my first "book," which was actually my
master's thesis. Because it is bound, has a hard cover, and sits on
my bookshelf, I consider it a book. The only people who have read
it are a few dedicated family members and supporters and my grad
school advisors but, hey, it's a book that I wrote. The book you
are reading right now is my second, coming almost twenty years
later, after many years as a pediatric speech-language pathologist
(SLP) and a little more than a decade of being a mom. My master's
thesis was titled "Who Are You Going to Turn To? An Assess-
ment of Communication Resources Used by Families of Children
with Autism Spectrum Disorders." I was interested in how people
navigate disability way back then, having no idea that I would
someday be a mom navigating the diagnoses of her own children,
who represent disability and neurodivergence. At the time, I was
a participant in a grant project at the University of Kansas that
centered on autism, and a condition of the funding was that my
graduate research had to be autism related. I find it fortuitous that

the topic of my thesis centered around the power of sources, in regard to how they shape perceptions.

Being Dan and Pete's mom has given me many opportunities to informally educate others about their disabilities, as well as about ableism. I found that I enjoy not only learning more about disability and ableism but also passing on what I learn to others.

Defining Ableism

Let's start with defining *ableism* to clarify what we are learning about and empowering our children to reject. In her book *Sitting Pretty: The View from My Ordinary Resilient Disabled Body*, Rebekah Taussig defines ableism in a way that is truer and more thorough than any other definition I have read. She writes:

> Ableism is the process of favoring, fetishizing, and building the world around a mostly imagined idealized body [and then] discriminating against those bodies perceived to move, see, hear, process, operate, look, or need differently from that vision. Often, the greater the deviation, the greater the discrimination.

Ableism is the misunderstanding and mistreatment of humans whose bodies, ways of thinking, and/or ways of behaving exist outside of a "norm" that society has predetermined.

What Disability Means in This Book

An important tenet of this book is that individuality exists in people regardless of labels or diagnoses. There is no universal agreement on which diagnoses or conditions are considered disabilities, which are considered neurodivergence, which might be both, and which might be neither. For the sake of understanding the terminology in this book, *neurodivergent* defines someone whose brain processes, learns, and/or behaves differently from what is considered typical. The term I am using to identify people whose brains process, learn, and/or behave in typical fashion is *neurotypical*. Some neurodivergent people also identify as disabled, and some do not.

Whether a person identifies as disabled may be innately personal. The accounts included in this book are from people spanning a variety of human conditions, and the primary common factor is that they identify as disabled or report treatment that can be described as ableist. Separation occurs when we focus too much on categorizing or labeling, which would detract from the foundational message of this book. Diagnoses and labels can be of great importance, and this is not to diminish that importance. Rather, we want to avoid misclassifying people. Ableism can affect people regardless of how they identify, so labels aren't as important to the mission of this book. The key goal of this book is to improve the reader's understanding of the ways in which ableism shows up.

The first-person accounts include a variety of disabilities, and specific disabilities will be named in examples, but this book will not tell you how to know if someone is or is not disabled, or even which conditions are considered disabilities. Through my research, I have discovered that being knowledgeable about a specific disability does not translate to knowledge about ableism. This book will teach you about ableism and how to avoid it, which will benefit every human you interact with. People learning how to be less ableist will positively affect other people, whether they identify as disabled or not.

Though there is variability regarding how people identify themselves, because ableism is the construct that this book aims to dismantle, *disability/disabled* will be the primary descriptive terms used to encompass the marginalized community and individuals in this book. By choosing disability/disabled, it is not my intention to exclude anyone. If I include a specific disability in a story or example, it does not mean that every individual with that diagnosis identifies as disabled. It means that the person in the story relayed an experience of ableism and identified in a certain way. Much of the insight that contributed to this book is from people who identify as disabled, and therefore, *disability/disabled* are the terms that have been selected. I use *nondisabled* to refer to people not identifying as disabled or not commonly affected by ableism. In specific chapters, when there is a reason to use additional terms, the terms will be explained.

Models of Disability

Many who are reading this will, at least initially, be operating from the medical model of disability, which attributes disability to a feature of the person and is caused by disease, health conditions, or trauma. I am writing this book as a person who primarily subscribes to the social model of disability. The social model of disability states that disabled people are disabled by society and manifestations of ableism, such as a lack of access and accommodations, rather than by their bodies or diagnoses. The social model was developed by disabled people and is the most widely accepted among disabled people. There will be additional information about models of disability in the book, with examples to support understanding.

Based on what I have learned from disabled voices, I have attempted to make a list of forms of ableism that are commonly reported. I have also attempted to glean, from these reported experiences, the insight, knowledge, and advice that they share and their preferences regarding ways to be supportive in simple and straightforward terms.

The Importance of Disabled Voices

In her book *Being Heumann*, disabled activist Judy Heumann writes about a rally outside a federal building in San Francisco on April 5, 1977, where disabled activists and allies met before occupying the offices of the Department of Health, Education, and Welfare. Judy recalls that Ed Roberts, another disabled activist at the rally, proclaimed, "Only we decide what is right for us." "Nothing about us without us" is a slogan commonly used in the disabled community. Making a commitment to listen and learn from disabled adults through their memoirs and social media pages has taught me so much and put many new and important considerations on my radar. I encourage everyone reading this book to do the same. Diversifying the voices you listen to and seeking guidance from disabled people are actionable steps toward confronting your own ableism.

No Shame, Only Growth

In the absolutely wonderful, award-winning short film *My Dad Matthew* by Wild Asparagus Productions, we learn about a disabled man named Matthew Wangeman. In the film, Matthew's young son Elijah says:

> All the assumptions and all the things we see as disabilities, or how we see people with disabilities, comes from our culture. It doesn't come from any other place, it comes from just how we've grown up, and that means that we can change that. We can see people in different ways.

That is the good news for anyone reading this book. Please remember that our culture has fed us the misconceptions that fuel ableism, so when you read about a form of ableism and realize you have engaged in it, try to avoid feelings of shame, guilt, or defensiveness. The fact that you have been ableist does not make you a bad person; rather, it makes you a person who has absorbed what our culture has saturated you in. I have been guilty of much, if not all, of the ableism included in this book and still have work to do. As Maya Angelou said, *You did what you knew how to do. And when you knew better, you did better.*

If you are reading this, it means you are open to knowing better and guiding your children to do better.

Inclusion, and Going Beyond

Inclusion is a buzzword that has been commonly used to describe what nondisabled people should strive for when it comes to disabled people. Disabled people have historically been excluded from society and subjected to mistreatment. In addition, mistruths were fabricated to fit historical narratives and, unfortunately, have continued to be passed down generationally. Inclusion has been sold culturally as the gold standard. It is my opinion, however, that inclusion is now the bare minimum. Disability advocates have fought hard for decades to be included, and thankfully, there are now some laws in place that are supposed to ensure inclusion.

But inclusion only combats exclusion and only goes as far as "We are allowing you in this space." It does not do anything to negate the many other forms of ableism that are outlined in this book. If inclusion is allowing space at the table, anti-ableism is removing all the barriers at the table that negatively affect a person's ability to participate. This book seeks to exist alongside the work of many disability advocates, to make a case to go beyond inclusion to an understanding of ableism and a commitment to dismantling it. There are ideas and strategies included that are specific to parents, but much of the information in this book can also be used by anyone who wants to learn more about ableism.

What to Expect in This Book

Each chapter starts with explanations and examples of the form of ableism being highlighted. Manifestations of each form of ableism are noted and explained individually. Each manifestation includes a "Challenge Yourself" section that provides some practical ideas and considerations that might help you navigate the manifestation addressed. For many manifestations, there is also information specific to educating your kids.

I close each chapter with a "Bring It Home" section that includes a summary of the chapter takeaways and a resource or two that you can bring home, figuratively or literally, to assist you in educating and nurturing anti-ableist conviction in your children. These sections include a quote or quotes from a children's book or two that relate to the information in that chapter.

It is my hope that wrapping up each chapter with examples of children's resources that already exist will help you feel empowered and provide options to bring these concepts home. You will find a list of those resources, as well as additional children's books, in the "Books for Your Child's Library" section at the end of this book, in case you would like to check them out from the library or add them to your home collection. Please consider pursuing some of these resources to meet the goal of dismantling your own internalized ableism and raising children who go beyond inclusivity to reject ableism. Finally, on the last page of the book, you will find a guide that can be used for personal reflection. It was created to be used with each chapter to deepen your learning.

You might be thinking, *I thought I bought a book that was going to teach my kids how to be nonableist. It sounds like this book includes a lot of work for me.* This book will give you some tools and ways to talk about disability with your kids, but your kids are going to have questions. If you are shaky and lack confidence in your basic

understanding of ableism—and haven't yet done any work to deconstruct ableism in yourself—you will struggle to answer their questions
or might inadvertently answer them in ways that perpetuate more
ableism. Being equipped to guide your children through something as
complex and deeply ingrained as our society's views of disability will
require a commitment to deepening your understanding. Thank you
for making the commitment to go beyond inclusion and do the work
to create change within yourself and, thus, generationally through
your children.

1

"THE AMAZING BOY WHO PUT ON HIS SHOES"

THE PRESUMPTION OF INCOMPETENCE

ONE AFTERNOON, I was standing in the hallway outside Dan's kindergarten classroom. He was changing from his boots into his shoes, which is something that happens several times per day for the six months of winter when you live in Minnesota. At a very young age, Minnesota kids develop the ability to independently cover their entire body in winter gear prior to embarking on snow play, and then come inside and take it all off. It's really quite remarkable.

Anyway, as Dan put on his shoes, a parent who was nearby with his own child putting on their shoes looked at me and said, "He's amazing."

I had only been Dan's mom for about a year and a half at this point. I was still in an early stage of learning how to be an ally and had plenty of internalized ableism that had still not yet been confronted. I knew enough to know that it was a misguided comment, but I considered the intent to be more important than the impact.

I felt I had to say something, because I knew Dan was listening and I did not want him to think that I did not agree. I was unprepared, though, to respond in a way that conveyed that I do, in fact, think he is amazing, with the caveat that it is not because he can put on his shoes. I awkwardly said, "You are pretty amazing, aren't you, Dan?" Dan was sitting still, which is what happens when he is carefully listening or in a state of contemplation. After five seconds or so, he said, "I'm an amazing piano player, right, Mom?" His response was pure—he went right for one of the things that is amazing about him, not thinking for a moment that it would be "putting on shoes while blind." This response from him taught me so much. He has been, and continues to be, one of my most influential teachers.

———————

Don't mistake this story as me discounting someone's ability to put on their shoes. This is a personal feat for some and is something to be celebrated in certain circumstances. But the key to understanding what is and is not a feat for someone is knowing them personally. For a stranger to determine that my son, a stranger to him, is amazing for putting on his shoes means that the stranger is making assumptions about what disabled people can and cannot do.

In *Love That Max*, "a blog about kids with disabilities who kick butt," a parent of a child with cerebral palsy writes about an encounter with a stranger at the swimming pool. She first writes about how she is proud of her son for many feats that might seem small to others.

> And yet: There are times when people who don't know our family, or Max, marvel over him, and it's made me uncomfortable. This past summer, Max was splashing around in a pool and a mom standing nearby said, "I just wanted to

tell you, your son is *amazing*." I mean, *I* know that years ago he was terrified of pools and he overcame his fears, and years ago he couldn't keep his balance but now he ambles around in the water, but *she* didn't know all that. She just saw a kid with disabilities splashing in a pool, seemingly qualifying him for an Olympic medal.

The strangers in these example encounters, Dan's and Max's, were very well intentioned, but they were operating from one of the most common and damaging manifestations of ableism: the Presumption of Incompetence. The Presumption of Incompetence tells us that we should not expect disabled people to be able to do much of anything, because they are not capable or competent by virtue of being disabled. It tells the lie that being disabled limits people in such a way that their ability to complete even menial tasks is a feat worthy of great elation.

In a brilliant video by Ryan Chamley called *Jeremy the Dud*, the main character, Jeremy, is twenty-one years old and described as a "dud." Jeremy is nonexceptional, meaning nondisabled and neurotypical. The show begins with him in an assisted-care apartment, completing normal morning tasks of daily living, such as making himself a bowl of cereal and brushing his teeth. As he brushes his teeth, a computerized voice directs him to "Gently move the brush back and forth in short strokes" and "brush the outer surfaces." In the community, he wears a tag to demonstrate his "without specialty" designation. As he seeks employment, since he has been discharged from assisted care due to age, he faces the Presumption of Incompetence. It is assumed that he will fulfill one of a few specific jobs, such as "wheelchair pusher" or "bottom wiper." When he expresses that he wants to look for a "normal job," his cousin, who is a double amputee—as most all the other characters in the show have a disability—says, "I'm all for dreaming big, but why would someone hire you?"

Jeremy the Dud uses humor to highlight many forms of ableism, including the Presumption of Incompetence, but when people experience this form of ableism in the real world, it is far from funny. In *A Face for Picasso*, Ariel Henley's memoir about growing up and living with a genetic condition called Crouzon syndrome that causes facial differences, Ariel writes about attending a cheerleading camp as a child. After being laughed at and mocked by peers and told "you don't look like a cheerleader, cheerleaders are supposed to be pretty," she explains how the camp leaders responded.

> After warm-ups, we were divided into groups by age. The woman in charge of the program called Zan and me over to her. "We are going to have you girls come over here." We followed the woman to a section of grass where the five- through seven-year-olds were learning an easier routine. Even though we were eleven and preparing to enter middle school, the woman told us it would be more appropriate for us to learn with them. The gesture was cloaked in a fake kindness and felt like a mix of passive aggression and a full-blown slap to the face. I was embarrassed and angry, because though the other kids were the ones to *say* we didn't look like cheerleaders, the adults—the ones who were supposed to know better—believed it.

A dear friend of mine shared with me how the Presumption of Incompetence affected her in a very impactful way.

> I got my bachelor's degree in San Francisco and decided to major in speech and language pathology. I had just come out of a very tough couple of years as a person who stuttered but then felt reborn with the help of a fantastic therapist and group therapy experience. Deciding to become a speech

therapist felt like an intimate need for me. My main professor in college was a tough, older lady who seemed not to like me from the very beginning. One day while meeting with her during office hours, she told me, "Summer, I really think this profession will be too hard for you. Your stutter is so severe, I worry it will only hinder you if you get through this program and maybe hinder patients looking for fluency." Her words stung and stuck with me from that day on. Being a young, impressionable student who definitely wasn't confident in herself at the time, I quickly found myself failing the program (specifically her classes) and eventually changed majors. I always look back and wonder, if she hadn't said those words, if I had been more confident in myself, if I knew then what I know now about being a person who stutters, would I have pushed through and made it as a speech pathologist? Probably. I did learn one important thing: words matter, whether you stutter or not. Words are impactful.

A personal note about my dear friend Summer: she is a gem of a human, and clients who stutter would have been lucky to have her as an SLP. When we exclude, we miss out on all that the excluded humans have to offer. That can extend all the way to friendship. Often, incompetence is presumed socially, and disabled people, children and adults alike, aren't given the opportunity to participate in authentic friendships. In her memoir *Just Human*, Arielle Silverman talks about how the way her peers saw her affected her socially.

I also became aware of how my peers treated me compared with how they treated each other. On the surface, most kids were nice. They would sit with me at lunch, and accept my invitations to play at my house after school. But the friendships only went so far. Only one friend, my best friend Liz, invited me to spend the night at her house on the weekends. Conversations were superficial, and sometimes it seemed my friends were afraid to get too close to me. I observed how my sister interacted with her friends, the good-natured teasing and sharing that went on between them. Rarely did my friends open up to me in the same way. Sometimes it seemed my classmates were more interested in helping me than in being my friend. Eventually, I came to attribute this behavior to my blindness, at least in part.

The Presumption of Incompetence can have damaging effects that extend beyond emotional distress for many people. Exclusion, underexposure, and lack of opportunity can have short- and long-term consequences. If someone has never been given the opportunity to learn a skill, they will not learn how to do it. This perpetuates the misconception of incompetence: the person cannot do the skill not because of actual incompetence but because of the lack of opportunity. In addition, being given the message that you are not capable can have a meaningful psychological impact. A 2012 study by Doren, Gau, and Lindstrom titled "The Relationship Between Parent Expectations and Postschool Outcomes of Adolescents with Disabilities" found that

> parent expectations related to graduating from high school with a standard diploma, obtaining a paid job, and attending postsecondary education after high school or both obtaining a job and attending postsecondary education were each significantly and positively associated with the likelihood that adolescents with disabilities would achieve these outcomes.

If the presumption of competence is a powerful influencer, then so is the Presumption of Incompetence.

What Does This Look Like in Action? Manifestations of the Presumption of Incompetence

1. Talking about a disabled person instead of talking to the person

This commonly happens to people in restaurants, among many other places. Many disabled adults share stories of a server or food service worker asking a friend or family member for their order instead of asking them directly. I have personally witnessed this happen to my son quite frequently when we are in public settings. Children that we don't know rarely talk directly to him without first asking me some sort of question about him. I direct them to talk to him instead of me. As an SLP, I have noticed that this also seems to happen frequently to people who use forms of communication other than mouth speaking.

Challenge Yourself

Talk directly to disabled people just as you talk to everyone else. If someone is limited in their ability to communicate, a person with them may assist or they may use alternative methods to respond. Another scenario is that they might not respond. Even if they don't respond, it is still a sign of respect to talk *to* a human rather than *about* them in their presence. All humans deserve the dignity of being addressed.

2. Assisting when assistance hasn't been requested

When Dan was younger and learning to do new things independently, there were many instances when I had to sternly tell people to refrain from doing things for him. One time at an indoor play place, he and I had discussed the route to the basketballs, which were his favorite at the time. I told him to head on over and I would be there in a few minutes. He set off on his way and, of course, was doing great.

And then, a well-meaning but assuming parent stopped him. I watched as they chatted and, before I knew it, the parent was looking around for the obviously negligent parent who allowed her blind child to travel alone, holding his hand and leading him to the basketballs. In this case, I walked over, told the parent that he was indeed capable of finding the basketballs on his own, and thanked the parent for the concern. The level of awkwardness was off the charts, as it typically is in these kinds of situations. I am often left with the feeling that the self-delegated helper found me forceful and unappreciative of their help.

Something I have always found humorous is the moment when strangers realize that Dan is blind as he maneuvers the upper levels of a play structure. There is a look of realization that comes across their face, followed by panic. They frantically look around for his "keeper" while sometimes positioning themselves under drop-offs near where he is playing, seemingly ready to catch him if he falls.

Their intentions, of course, are rooted in the spirit of helpfulness but are driven by the Presumption of Incompetence. That presumption means their impact is the opposite of helpful. Though I am thankful for the spirit of helpfulness and looking out for each other, I rarely notice parents doing this for nondisabled children. I have heard many blind adults share their stories about times a stranger decided they were incapable of crossing the street safely and took it upon themselves to (a) grab them (the first inexcusable act) and then (b) pull them across the street, despite protests on their part. Even when a stranger is unsuccessful in forcing their help, the blind person can end up in a state of disorientation as a result of the scuffle. Any pertinent landmarks that had been used might be unclear, which can put the person in a position of danger because of the stranger who tried to force their help.

People often put themselves into the "noble rescuer" role and can become defensive when they are called out. When people truly need help, heroics are heroic. But, in most cases, disabled people do not need rescuing. They might need a little extra time, accessibility, or accommodation, but they should be the ones in control of determining what they need.

This can also sometimes manifest through disabled people being supervised and "checked on" more often than nondisabled people. Dan has complained to me about people at his school asking him where his para* is when he is traveling at school. He says it has happened a few times with adults but happens mostly with peers. It isn't uncommon to see police and security personnel approaching disabled people to check on them even when they are not showing signs of distress. The spirit of helpfulness is positive, but when it is assumed that disabled people need help at a disproportionate rate, it is indicative of ableism.

Challenge Yourself

Assume that people, disabled or not, do not need help unless they ask or you see obvious signs that they do. Do not assume that a person needs help just because they are disabled and don't navigate situations or exist in the same way that you do. If you are concerned because of factors specific to the situation, ask the person. It can be as simple as a greeting and a check-in. "Hi. Is everything OK?"

3. Social exclusion

A child who uses a wheelchair might not be invited to a party at a play place or playground due to assumptions being made about his ability to participate physically. An intellectually disabled child might not be given the option to participate in extracurricular activities such

---

* *Para* is short for *paraprofessional*, a school employee who provides support for a disabled student, under the supervision of a licensed teacher.

as school plays, book club, or LEGO club due to assumptions about her abilities. Ariel Henley's story from cheer camp is an example of social exclusion, as Ariel and her sister were not allowed to participate in the same activities as the other children their age.

Challenge Yourself

Be both clear about the details of the event or opportunity and inclusive, even if you are unsure if someone will want to participate. The power to decide should always be in the hands of the individual. If the person indicates an interest in coming, do everything possible to provide accommodations and accessibility. The parents of many of Dan's friends have done a beautiful job of this by not assuming he will or will not want to participate and by asking what they can do to create an inclusive experience for him. It can be as simple as "So-and-so wants to invite Dan to his birthday party. It will be at such-and-such place and we will be doing ABC before doing XYZ. Let me know if he is interested in coming and if there is anything we can do to ensure his ability to participate." By simply modeling inclusion along with a willingness to accommodate, you will teach your kids how to be supportive and inclusive.

Treat every child as a child who has the opportunity to participate in an event and do everything you can to make sure they can join the fun if they choose to. I have a personal goal to extend accommodation invitations to everyone when hosting events. When creating an invitation to an event, it seems pretty easy to include a line such as "With RSVP, please indicate accommodation and access barriers that need to be considered." This simple line means no people are singled out or put in the position to have to speak up about needs not knowing how they will be received. As a parent, if I saw this in an invitation, I would feel very comfortable reaching out to the inviting party with questions and suggestions.

4. Opportunity exclusion

When someone is excluded from opportunities because of disability, it can lead to feelings of shame and inadequacy. When Pete was eight and in the second grade, we didn't know yet that he was dyslexic, but he was starting to notice that reading and writing were much harder for him than they seemed to be for his peers. Unbeknownst to his dad and me, Pete had indicated interest in a program at his school called Independent Investigation, referred to as I.I., that some of his classmates had been participating in. I.I. allows students to be pulled out of class to work on an interest-based project that they later share with their classmates. After he asked his teacher if he could do I.I., a staff member asked him to read something, and when he couldn't, he was told that he was not ready to participate in I.I. The following weekend, he told his dad that he wanted to create a poster about alligator snapping turtles. He and his dad researched and recorded facts, found and printed pictures, and even made little clay models of what the alligator snapping turtle eats. When he was finished, I lauded him for such a cool project. He wasn't as proud as I would've expected but instead was tense, and he responded by saying, "My teacher said I couldn't do I.I. because I can't read, so I can show her that I don't even need to do it at school because I can just do it at home."

My jaw dropped. I had no idea about I.I. or about this experience that had caused him to feel such inadequacy. I told him I was really proud of him for pursuing his interest in the project at home even though he had faced a barrier in another setting, and I asked if he wanted to take it to school to show his class. Initially he said yes but later changed his mind.

He and I revisited this experience when I asked if it was all right if I shared it in the book. He said, "If I had the confidence then that I have now, I would have walked that poster right into my classroom and said, 'See? I *can* do it.'"

Though our son seemingly "overcame" the adversity of the situation, it certainly did not mean he escaped the impacts of the feelings of inadequacy and shame that resulted from this exclusion. These feelings are common when a person is considered incompetent, as many dyslexic people are judged to be, because of the stigma and stereotypes attached when someone is not a good speller or fluent reader. The Presumption of Incompetence creates opportunity exclusion for countless people, across all demographic groups, every single day.

Challenge Yourself

Every individual should be given the chance to decide what they are and are not interested in and should be given the chance to attend, try, apply, and prove themself the same as those who have not been presumed incompetent by virtue of disability. If someone needs support to participate, make it a priority. If excluding someone on the basis of lacking prerequisite skills, examine these prerequisite skills to ensure that they are necessary, and to see if they can be modified to include the support that would make the opportunity accessible to more people.

5. Social inauthenticity

The Presumption of Incompetence can lead to a drastic reduction in organic social opportunities. When Dan was freshly five, he and I were at a play place. While exploring near a peer, he came upon a toy that another child was playing with. He started to take the toy, and the child who was playing with it, justifiably, held on to it and attempted to pull it back. A preschool tug-of-war was taking place, which is a common occurrence with small children. In this instance, though, the response of the other parent was different. I was talking to my son, explaining that the other child had the toy first and that we could wait for a turn with the toy. He was displeased with this answer, as you can imagine. Soon, the other child's parent rushed over and told her daughter to "let him have it." I said, "No, she had it first. I'm helping my son understand that we are going to give it back and wait for a turn." The parent said, "That's OK. He can just have it," removed the toy from her daughter's hand, and led her daughter away.

I know this parent was trying to be nice, but this reaction was problematic for a few reasons. One is that it denied my son the opportunity to learn about social interactions organically. I often find it difficult for Dan to learn how to get along with others we are not close to or well acquainted with, because others rarely act the same with him and rarely expect the same behavior from him as from nondisabled peers. My son is, and has been, capable of learning the ins and outs of social interaction and friendship but is rarely given opportunities to learn.

I want to note that, according to another child's individual circumstances, this might have been a helpful way to handle a situation. Situations like these with strangers can be difficult to gauge, and your initial instinct might be what is most helpful. Similar to the discussion of Dan putting on his shoes, though, the automatic assumption that a child cannot handle these kinds of social situations because they are disabled is ableist.

In our situations, I always explain what is actually best, but I usually get the "No, it's OK," with the outcome that doesn't allow for it to be the learning opportunity that it could be. The other parent and child rush off before I can make a case to the contrary. There have been a few times when the parent allows me to take the lead but then backpedals when my son has a hard time with the expectation. He does have a really heartbreaking sad face, but I'd argue that most kids have heartbreaking sad faces. What my son has learned from this is that he isn't held to the same expectations as others, because it is presumed that he can't handle the typical social expectations for his age. If a child isn't allowed to learn the give-and-take of friendship, he may end up unable to maintain friendships in his future because his social experiences and responses have been so atypical. In addition, when he is denied the opportunity to feel hard feelings related to social interaction, how will he ever learn how to process and manage them?

Challenge Yourself

Resist assumptions that lead you to treat a child differently in social situations because of their disability. If you are unsure of what is helpful in the moment, just ask. It can be as simple as "Let me know what is most helpful from me/my child right now. I'll follow your lead." This is probably ideal all the time and not just with disabled children. All children have a hard time sometimes, and in most cases, caregivers know what will and won't be helpful in any given situation.

Avoid scolding your children for advocating for themselves in a disagreement with a disabled child if you would not be scolding them if the child were nondisabled. Having a different standard that is based on assumptions about a disabled person is ableism—and being scolded for interacting with a disabled child might make a child anxious or reluctant to interact in the future due to being treated differently for a response that is typical for them. Try to be consistent in what you expect from your children, unless you have additional information from the disabled child or his family that guides you otherwise.

If the other child gets upset, like my son did in the example with the toy, try to avoid making assumptions if you debrief with your child afterward. Use what you know and be direct. "That little boy got upset because he wanted to play with the toy that you had. You had it first, so he had to wait for his turn. It's hard to wait, isn't it?" If you are looking to model compassion in situations like this, you could take an additional step and talk about how we sometimes feel sad for people when they feel sad or when they are struggling. In the situation noted earlier, Dan's disability had no influence on the situation, so connecting his feelings of frustration to his blindness would be inaccurate.

In regard to friendship inauthenticity, I want to make a few notes. On occasion, it has been suggested that inviting disabled kids to birthday parties is an act of charity. Let me be clear that when disabled kids are isolated socially, it is sad and unfortunate. They, like every child, would benefit from authentic friendships. Be sure to keep in mind, though, that a pity invitation is not a gesture of authentic friendship. If your child is having a birthday party and is asked to select a few friends to attend, please don't demand that your child invite a disabled peer. If your child chooses to invite them, great! A way around this, if you wish to be inclusive, is to invite the entire class. But singling out a child for an invitation because they are disabled is another example of social inauthenticity.

This is just my opinion, and maybe there are parents out there who want their kids to be invited no matter what. But my preference as a parent is for my kids to have authentic friendships, even if it is only with a select few. There is no rule that having more close friends is better, and some children do better with a smaller group of close friends. Children who are invited out of pity will most likely pick up on the vibe of why they are there, and that isn't healthier for them than not being invited. That being said, inviting every child *but* the child with a disability is a situation you will want to dig into and unpack.

6. Exclusion from activities presumed to be too challenging

Someone being presumed incompetent can have health care implications as well and can leave a disabled person with an unmet need that they need to expend additional effort to resolve. A friend shared a personal story about a time he was presumed incompetent and not trusted when sharing the truths about his personal reality. He wrote:

I would prefer to keep this anonymous, or possibly use a pseudonym. I am too identifiable, and many of us disabled folks are wary of retaliation if by some chance a negative statement we made regarding a procedure or provider became public. This also shapes how/if we confront an issue. At times we may choose silence over the risk of calling a situation out knowing this could negatively impact care.

I identify as a blind cancer survivor. My eyes were enucleated shortly after my second birthday due to a rare childhood cancer. The greatest challenges I face in life are the ableist attitudes of those who fear blindness and view me as incompetent. I live in a world where such attitudes are the norm.

Six years ago I required a cardio stress test in preparation for treatment for a serious illness. This involves walking on a treadmill while measurements of heart function are monitored. I arrived to the facility where the exam would take place, unconcerned about the procedure. I have been a runner for many years. Walking on a treadmill for five or ten minutes is minor for me.

I was therefore taken unawares when the technician began raising concerns about my ability to walk on the treadmill. She called in her supervisor for consultation. The supervisor was terrified that I might fall off the treadmill resulting in grave injury. I was informed that I was a liability risk and she would not allow the procedure to continue. I was unprepared for such foolishness, but must always be prepared for such foolish notions. I am usually able to calm people such as this and help them get back on track. The more I tried to calm her down with facts—my marathon in 2005, forty years of running, etc.—the more frantic she became. I finally requested that the electrodes be removed from my chest and my shirt be returned to me. I informed them on the way out the door that I would be in touch with legal counsel by day's end. I think they thought I was blowing off steam. I was doing no such thing. Their ableist attitudes were preventing me from moving forward with a critical treatment. My life could depend upon clearing this up. Given a choice, I would not have pursued the matter, but I had no choice.

My friend is a grown adult who has decades of lived experience in his body, and yet, because of his disability, was presumed incompetent to complete a task that he had completed many times over. His presumed incompetence left important questions unanswered until he put forth the time and energy to seek out health care providers who wouldn't allow ableism to create barriers to his care.

Challenge Yourself

Listen to disabled people when they tell you what they are and are not capable of. Presuming incompetence and then not listening when a person defends their competence is a double punch of ableism.

Bring It Home

In the children's book *We'll Paint the Octopus Red* by Stephanie Stuve-Bodeen, the main character is notified that her baby brother has arrived. She shares all the plans she has made for herself and her brother, including teaching him how to paint an octopus. Big sister then finds out that her brother has Down syndrome and starts to guess that it means her brother won't be able to do all the things she has planned.

"Then he won't be able to paint the octopus." My dad said that he was positive Isaac could do that if I showed him how.

After voicing her speculations to her dad, and having her dad reassure her, she goes on:

> By the time we were done talking, we couldn't find one of those million things that Isaac wouldn't be able to do with me. "If Isaac has this Down thing, then what can't he do?" My dad hugged me. He said that as long as we were patient with Isaac, and helped him when he needed it, there probably wasn't anything he couldn't do.

It is important to model the presumption of competence to our kids throughout our interactions. In educating your kids about disabled populations, you can casually talk about how they use their adaptive equipment or accommodations to competently live their lives. The way things are done might look different, but a person doing something in a different way is still competent and able.

Examples include: "He uses his hands to make signs, which are similar to the words that we speak with our mouths, to communicate with others." "She uses her wheelchair to go do the things that we do on our legs." "They use their prosthetic hand to do the same things that we do with our hands, like eating, driving, and writing."

In the book *Island of the Mix-Ups* by Dusty Buell, an elephant and monkey from the Jungle of Ordinary make their way to a new island where they find new friends with differences they had never imagined, like an animal with a lion body and elephant trunk who can climb trees and pick bananas with his trunk.

> For a while he and Wally hung out with the Mix-ups and found themselves having fun playing the games of this new

place. They soon realized this island was very similar to their own. The Mix-ups did the same type of thing, though often in different ways. It didn't take very long for Tusk and Wally to work out that there can be more than one correct way of doing something.

2

"YOU'RE SO BRAVE"

DISABILITY AS AN INSPIRATION

WHEN YOU THINK about how disability is represented socially, what comes to mind? Whether it is the disabled character in the TV show or movie who overcomes her treacherous disability to meet her goal, the news story about the player on the team who has a disability and makes a big shot in the game, or the disabled child at your kid's school who is lauded as the community hero, none of us are strangers to inspiration being perpetually tied to disability.

Stella Young was a disabled woman and revolutionary disability rights activist. Her 2014 TED Talk titled "I'm Not Your Inspiration, Thank You Very Much" is a highly recommended resource that will help you better understand Disability as an Inspiration. Young explains:

> I am not here to inspire you. I am here to tell you that we have been lied to about disability. We've been sold the lie that disability is a Bad Thing. Capital B, capital T. It's a bad

thing and to live with a disability makes you exceptional.

It's not a bad thing and it doesn't make you exceptional.

Young coined the term *inspiration porn* and defined it as the objectification of disabled people for the benefit of nondisabled people. She gives a few examples of inspiration porn, showing images of disabled children participating in common physical activities, like playing soccer, with accompanying phrases like "The only disability is a bad attitude." She notes that the children in the pictures are simply using their bodies to the best of their capacity to engage in activities that aren't out of the ordinary, just as all of us do.

She goes on to ask, "So is it really fair to objectify them, in the way that we do? To share those images?"

Disability as an Inspiration is one of the most common forms of ableism and, as Stella Young explained, tells us the lie that being disabled is such a hardship and enduring it such a grand feat that, by default, it makes the disabled person inspirational. Disability as an Inspiration serves the purpose of making the able-bodied feel better about our own circumstances. It tells us that disabled people bring us warm fuzzies, regardless of their individual circumstances or if they themselves are seeking to provide, or share in, the warm fuzzies.

My guess is that most people either haven't taken the time to question if being used as an inspiration is acceptable to disabled people, or assume that disabled people who are used as inspiration aren't bothered by it. Many disabled people, however, report being uncomfortable with Disability as an Inspiration.

In an April 2016 article titled "Please Stop Calling My Life with a Disability 'Inspiring,'" from the *Establishment* and found on Medium, journalist Venessa Parekh shares how it makes her feel when people use her for inspiration.

> When I'm getting into the bus—usually in a little panic because I'm running late—and the kindly woman sitting by the door nods vigorously and smiles "well done" at me, it doesn't brighten my day. This wasn't a trapeze act; I just wheeled up a pretty solid ramp, extended by a flick of the kindly bus driver's finger, and into an empty space.

I wonder if that woman cheered for each person who used their legs to walk up the steps into the bus, too.

On the episode "Disabled NOT Differently Abled" of the podcast *Two Hot Takes*, guest Molly Burke, disabled content creator and speaker, talks about being told that she is an inspiration simply for existing as disabled.

> I mean, the amount of times that I am told when I am out, just like grabbing my coffee at Starbucks, "You're so brave. You're so inspiring." And I'm like . . . Um, you don't know anything about me other than the fact that I'm disabled. Like, I could be a drug dealer. I'm not. But I could be. You don't know what I've done in my life. I could be such a jerk. You don't know. I could be the high school bully. You don't know that I'm an inspiration, just for existing. If you know my story, if you know everything that I have been through which, granted, is a damn lot, you can say I'm inspiring. Because I have had to fight through even more than many in my own community. So, like, if you find what I have overcome inspiring, I am happy to be that for you. I am not happy to be inspiring for you by simply existing and getting my coffee.

In addition to disabled people being deemed inspirational just for existing, acts of kindness extended to disabled people are also often deemed an inspiration and portrayed differently from acts of kindness that occur among the able-bodied.

In *A Face for Picasso*, Ariel Henley writes about a time when she, her twin sister, and their nondisabled best friend were given an award to "commend their inspiring behavior," thanked for being examples of kindness and resilience, and praised for inspiring their school community to be more kind to one another. Their certificates said Most Inspirational on them. They started to wonder why they were inspirational. After much pondering and processing, Ariel asked her therapist, "Was Nina given an award simply for being friends with Zan and me? Because being friends with the *ugly* girls that everyone else treated as lepers was inspiring?"

In a November 2019 article written by Sarah Levis, "Inspiration Porn: Once You See It, You Can't Not See It," she outlines some common examples of Disability as an Inspiration: "How wonderful the football player is for asking the poor disabled girl to prom" and "How gracious it was for the basketball team to make a disabled boy's dream come true by letting him take a shot at the basketball game."

In these situations, the things that happened aren't negative and naturally bring about good feelings. But if, when we talk about them, we objectify the disabled individual for the sake of making others feel better about themselves, then we are perpetuating Disability as an Inspiration.

David Perry, history professor and disability scholar, talks about how Disability as an Inspiration is often perpetuated not in actual interactions but, rather, in the media response to those interactions and the way we ourselves talk about them. In an *Establishment* article posted on Medium in February 2016, "How 'Inspiration Porn' Reporting Objectifies People with Disabilities," Perry writes:

> In almost every case, I have no criticisms of the young men
> and women who are seeking ways to better include their

classmates with Down Syndrome or other intellectual disabilities. Teenagers . . . are good people looking for ways to be more inclusive. High-school kids must take steps because too often, our education systems, recreation leagues and society at large lack natural pathways for people with and without disabilities to compete, play, or develop easy social interactions with each other. My issue is with the reporting.

If you pay attention and reflect on stories often shared on social media and by mainstream media outlets, it will be easy to find examples of Disability as an Inspiration perpetuated.

What Does This Look Like in Action? Manifestations of Disability as an Inspiration

1. Connecting disabled people with inspirational messages

One manifestation of Disability as an Inspiration is the use of pictures, videos, or depictions of disabled people participating in activities with attached words or discussion that are meant to invoke feelings of awe or inspiration. The idea behind these is that you have it easy by virtue of being nondisabled. "What's your excuse?" "What are you complaining about?" I have seen these in gyms, locker rooms, and other spaces where people are seeking motivation to excel in physical performance. Additional examples include people stacking a disabled person's circumstances against their own in an expression of gratitude and referencing being more or less fortunate. "I can't even imagine how hard that must be. I'll never complain again." "I was given two legs that work; I need to be grateful." When people do this, it seems their intent isn't to be insulting. I think it is assumed that disabled people find it to be a compliment or statement of acknowledgment.

In her TED Talk, Stella Young talks about using disabled people as inspiration and encourages the listeners to think about this from the perspective of the disabled person: "However bad my life is, it could be worse. I could be that person." She goes on: "What if you are that person?"

I find this simple way of thinking about Disability as an Inspiration to be very powerful. Being a metaphor for a pitiful existence wouldn't feel very good, would it?

Challenge Yourself

Reframe the way you think about disability to reject the implication of inspiration without individual circumstances. Don't perpetuate this form of ableism in the stories that you share. Any time you come across a disabled person's story, carefully evaluate what you are seeing and take the time to break it down. Ask yourself, *Is this person's disability being used to inspire me to appreciate my own circumstances?* If the answer is yes, acknowledge it as ableist and refrain from sharing or reinforcing it.

If your child is witness to this form of ableism, take the time to address it with them. Rather than just saying it's not OK, help them understand why.

2. Giving "inspiration" awards to disabled people

In an article for The Mighty titled "How to Avoid 'Inspiration Porn' When Talking About Disability,' Catherine S writes:

> I've been the subject of inspiration porn. One of my earliest "inspiration porn" memories is from my primary school days. There was a prize given at the end of each year. Without fail every year I would get an award for overcoming obstacles or perseverance. It was never explicitly stated what exactly I was

overcoming, but I knew they were referring to my disability. Everybody around me seemed thrilled. Everybody except me. While everybody around me was feeling inspired by the tenacious little disabled girl with a "can do" attitude, I wanted to run out of the building and hide. The awards emphasized my difference, and all I wanted was to be the same. They seemed to benefit those giving the award more than me.

In addition to *most inspirational*, other words that imply the same thing include *perseverance, determination, tenacity,* and *grit.* If the award is praising a disabled person for continuing to do life in their current state, it is linked to inspiration.

Challenge Yourself

Include disabled people in award recognitions, but make sure the award isn't ableist and is based on personal strengths, attributes, or performance. Don't single out disabled people for the purpose of rewarding them without giving careful thought to what you are rewarding them for. I have come across several stories of disabled people who have reflected on the experience of receiving an award not as a fond memory but rather as an embarrassing or traumatic event. Don't shy away from talking about the accomplishments of disabled people, but remember to check yourself first: Would you consider this an accomplishment for a nondisabled person? Is what you are rewarding the person for a quality attributed to their character or accomplishments that they recognize as accomplishments, or is it a version of Disability as an Inspiration?

3. Nondisabled associates as saints

Praising those who choose to associate and spend time with disabled people is another manifestation of Disability as an Inspiration. As a pediatric speech-language pathologist, I have had many people tell me that I am a "saint" for doing my job. I am not a saint. I get paid to provide a service, and the children I serve are consumers of a service, just the same as any other population who receives a service. Maybe I have been lucky, but my pediatric client base has been fairly easy to get along with and mostly respectful and reasonable. I can't report that every professional in a similar field would say the same thing, but the fact remains that there is as much variability in ease or difficulty in working with people from the disability community as from the nondisabled population. If you ask me, those who work in customer service are the real saints. Adult consumers in the twenty-first century can be pretty difficult sometimes.

In all seriousness, the notion that choosing to spend time with disabled people is an act of sainthood seems to be a common phenomenon, unfortunately. This implication is hurtful and ableist. It is another example of using disability as a way to make people feel better about themselves, suggesting that disabled people are unsavory to spend time with or laborious to interact with.

Many videos that include a high school student asking a disabled peer to prom go viral or make it to mainstream media. Rarely do similar stories about nondisabled students asking their nondisabled peers to prom get so much attention. Videos of disabled students being crowned homecoming king or queen also get much more attention than when a nondisabled student is crowned.

Is it ableist to choose to ask a disabled peer to a dance or to crown a disabled student as the homecoming royalty? Of course not. As David Perry mentioned, the ableism manifests itself in how we talk about it. The suggestion that the nondisabled students who chose or voted for a disabled peer are heroes is problematic, not the actual act of choosing or voting for them.

The foundation of this book is the belief that many parents wish for their children to be kind and inclusive to all. I believe this is why these moments feel powerful for so many. On the surface, they seem to be shining examples of kindness and gestures of inclusion. To be honest, they often are. But centering the nondisabled peers suggests that the disabled students' worthiness lies in the eyes of their peers and not in their inherent worth, which exists regardless of how their peers feel about them. We assume that the disabled kids are being rejected, probably because of all the ableism that we *know* is rampant, so when we see signs to the contrary, we celebrate. It comes from a good place. But unfortunately, ableism has twisted this into putting nondisabled peers who are kind and inclusive on a pedestal. We respond to one manifestation of ableism with another one. If someone is a saint for choosing you, there is an implication that you are unworthy or burdensome, which is the inverse of a disabled child receiving a message of unworthiness through being bullied or mistreated. The underlying message is the same and harmful either way.

When I watch these videos, I usually see clear evidence that the students who were chosen are completely beloved by their peers. It doesn't seem they were chosen out of pity. It seems they were chosen because they are loved. The excitement you see from the peers who voted, and the joy expressed as they celebrate, are clear signs that it was not an obligatory choice. None of that is bad. But then, the comments start. "Bless these kids!" "Oh, there is still good in the world!" The dark shadow of ableism moves in when we assign sainthood to the students who voted for a peer who happened to be disabled.

Challenge Yourself

Speak about your child's disabled peers the same way you speak about their nondisabled peers. There isn't any need to separate them. Don't praise your children for being friends with disabled children any more than you would praise them for being friends with someone nondisabled. Praise your children for acts of kindness and inclusivity in all situations and with all peers. For example, a child inviting a non-disabled friend to play is just as lovely as a child inviting a disabled friend to play. A child going out of their way to help a nondisabled peer pick up the contents of a spilled backpack is no less praiseworthy than a child helping a disabled peer in a similar situation. Treat the victories of your child's disabled peers no differently than you would if the peers were nondisabled. Avoiding the cultural norm of "weighing" kindness will help you steer your children away from developing misconceptions about disability and inspiration.

When you and your child witness stories shared in a way that center the nondisabled person as heroic and objectify the disabled person as inspirational, make sure to talk to your child about it. If you do not contextualize what children see, they will receive the ableism and, without someone negating it, might accept it as appropriate.

For example: "I wonder why the news is doing a story about two people going to a dance together. Lots of people are pairing up to go to the dance together, but they only did a story about these two. Why do you think they picked this story? What are they suggesting about the person with a disability if they think the person without a disability is a hero for asking her? Do you think that is true? How would you decide who to ask to a dance?"

4. Expecting disabled people to inspire us with their hardships

When it is determined that the most significant contribution a disabled person can make is to pour out their pain and hardship for society to consume, Disability as an Inspiration is at play.

In her 2021 book *Year of the Tiger: An Activist's Life*, Alice Wong prepares her readers for what to expect in her memoir while delivering a powerful message.

One of my concerns when writing *Year of the Tiger* was about the publishing industry's propensity to publish memoirs by disabled people as opposed to other types of book they might prefer to write. I don't have any numbers, but it seems there are more disabled people with memoirs than with graphic novels or cookbooks, with books of photography or poetry, or in genres such as speculative fiction, romance, children's literature, and *every single other category*. Why is that? Is it because readers expect disabled people to have an interest only in explaining disability rather than focusing on their other talents and passions? Is it because disability is more easily understood as an individual phenomenon without broader social and cultural contexts? Is it because it's more palatable and "humanizing" to learn about one person and the presumed challenges and adversities in their life? Is it because the reader expects a catharsis and warm, empathetic after-school-special fuzzies by the last page? *Is it because they sell?*

Challenge Yourself

When disabled people choose to share their experiences, their autonomy in that decision is important. Try to view these aspects of their story the same way you view experiences nondisabled people have faced in their lives. The adversity a disabled person faces is influential and shapes them in many ways, but that is true for adversity in general. We don't expect every nondisabled Tom, Dick, and Harry who we connect with at the office to tell us about the hardships they have faced. We don't wait for Tom, Dick, and Harry's hardship stories to decide if they have value. We allow Tom, Dick, and Harry to show us who they are and what they are good at through how they do their jobs, interact with others, and move through life. If Tom decides to share a personal story with you at the company holiday party, you understand him better but generally don't use that information for any other purposes. Don't expect a disabled person to reveal any personal information to earn respect, prove worthiness, or inspire you. If you are looking for examples of the adversity that disability can cause, there are numerous memoirs by people with disabilities that you can access.

Bring It Home

Teach your children about disabled people who have been truly inspirational by making significant contributions to society. You can learn a lot from a simple Google search. When you tell your child about these pioneers, *do not* use phrases like "despite their disability" or "they overcame their disability and went on to . . ." For example, saying "Despite being deaf, Thomas Edison transformed the world through his inventions" suggests that his deafness and inventing are somehow at odds with each other and that being deaf can negatively affect someone's ability to invent. To the contrary, Edison's motivation behind his innovation in inventing the phonograph was related to his disability. Efforts made to accommodate disability sometimes bring us new ideas and technologies that are widely beneficial.

Even though most disabilities do not prevent people from accomplishing great things, it is a common misconception that disabled people with impressive accomplishments somehow put their disabilities aside or conquered them. These pioneers were disabled while pioneering. Teaching our children to reject the idea that disability neither guarantees nor negates greatness is important to eliminating harmful misconceptions.

In addition, help your children understand that we all exist as individuals with unique attributes and that inspiration comes equally from disabled and nondisabled people. In the book *We're All Wonders* by R. J. Palacio, the main character has a facial difference and talks about what it is like to be a "wonder," as his mom refers to him. He says, "I know I can't change the way I look. But maybe, just maybe . . . people can change the way they see. If they do, they'll see that I'm a wonder. And they'll see that they're wonders, too. We're all wonders!"

3

"WHAT'S WRONG WITH YOU?"

DISABILITY AS A DEFICIT

I N HER BOOK *SITTING PRETTY*, Rebekah Taussig writes of a time she was trying to explain to her brother what she wanted the world to gain from her memoir.

> In the midst of my verbal wandering, I inevitably reached for the word "shame"—the box where I had lived for so very long, the box I still find myself tumbling back into with less provocation than I'd like to admit. This is the shame that attaches so easily to a body that doesn't fit, the shame that buds, blossoms, and consumes when you believe that your existence is a burden, a blemish, on the well-oiled machine of Society. I tried to explain to David how much I want my writing to meet people in that shame, to lift the veil and point to the source, to remind people that their disabled bodies are not The Problem here.

Disability as a Deficit tells us the lie that having a disability creates an automatic inadequacy. In an episode of *Open Stutter* on YouTube, guest Aliza talks about the emotional impact of her stutter being treated as a deficit. She explains that there are two types of stuttering, overt and covert. Overt stuttering is when others can observe someone stuttering, and covert stuttering is when a person is using strategies to avoid stuttering. A person who stutters covertly puts a great deal of energy into the strategies used to decrease or eliminate stuttering. Aliza mentions that when she tells people that she stutters, they tend to respond by praising her fluency. She says that as a person who strives to be more overt, this is hurtful.

> A stutter itself is really vulnerable just because you, it
> depends how you feel about it, in yourself. All the shame
> and judgment and embarrassment, it just makes it scarier
> to let people know, or to show them.

Why do we consider disability to be a deficit? As I mentioned in the introduction, disability has long been identified and viewed through the framework of the medical model, which attributes disability to a feature of the person's body, physical health, or mental health and is caused by disease, health conditions, or trauma. The medical model operates from a standard of health and wellness and pathologizes deviations from this standard. The medical model, by design, looks for a problem, and then includes a prescribed treatment to fix or alleviate the problem. Disabled people, like almost everyone in the world, receive and rely on medical care. Some disabled people have medical complexities and vulnerabilities that require more frequent and extensive medical care than what is average. I want to be clear that this is not a dis on modern medicine. Medical expertise and care is essential.

The medical model being the standard for how we identify disability, however, is considered by many disabled people to be inappropriate. Let's consider an example. The d/Deaf community has a complex relationship with the medical model.* The medical model of disability says that deafness is a deviation from a standard of health and looks for a cure or fix. In the case of deafness, the fix or medical intervention is a hearing aid or cochlear implant. Deaf individuals, when provided access and accommodation, live full and varied lives as members of society able to interact with hearing individuals as well as others in the Deaf community. These accommodations broaden not only the d/Deaf individuals' lives but also the lives of everyone they can now interact with. They don't need to be "fixed."

The Americans with Disabilities Act (ADA) definition of disability specifically notes limitations—and it is crucial to consider the source of a limitation in a disabled person's life. When considering disability through the social model, we can understand the powerful roles that access, accommodation, and supportive community play in reducing limitations. As Stella Young explains in her TED talk:

> Life as a disabled person is actually somewhat difficult; we do overcome some things. But the things that we're overcoming are not the things that you think they are. They are not things to do with our bodies. I use the term *disabled* quite deliberately, because I subscribe to what's called the social model of disability, which tells us that we are more disabled by the society that we live in than our bodies and our diagnoses.

Naoki Higashida was a teenager when he wrote the insights and reflections in the book *The Reason I Jump*, which was the inspiration for the documentary of the same name. Naoki shares:

---

* A terminology note: *Deaf* with a capital *D* describes people who identify as culturally Deaf and are engaged with the Deaf community. When a lowercase *d* is used, it simply refers to the physical nature of hearing loss.

When I was small, I didn't even know that I was a kid with special needs. How did I find out? By other people telling me I was different from everyone else, and that this was a problem.

In a TEDx talk called "Why Everything You Know About Autism Is Wrong," autistic scholar and researcher Jac den Houting says:

In 2011, when I was twenty-five years old, I was diagnosed with autism. And it wasn't a tragedy. It was the best thing that's ever happened to me. Finding out I'm autistic, it brought me an overwhelming sense of relief. My whole life up to that point finally made sense. My paradigm about myself shifted. I wasn't a failed neurotypical person. I was a perfectly good autistic person.

She goes on to talk about what happened when she started learning about autism, before she got her PhD and became a researcher.

I was bombarded with information. I was bombarded with information about my deficits. Autism causes deficits in social interaction. Deficits in communication. Restrictive and repetitive behaviors. Sensory processing deficits. For me, that information just didn't make sense. Finding I'm autistic had completely changed my life for the better. How could something that was so positive for me be such a bad thing?

Disabled people are generally made keenly aware that their disability is viewed as a deficit and, as a result, spend a great deal of energy on making sense of the discrepancy between what they are being told and what they feel to be true for them.

In the book *NeuroTribes*, Steve Silberman talks about Carol Greenberg, an autistic mother of an autistic child and contributor to the website Thinking Person's Guide to Autism. She explained how her son once communicated to his parents that he wanted them to "light candles." They initially worried that he was developing an interest in fire. When a medical condition or diagnosis has been presented as a defect, it is a common reaction to assume the worst. Then, they heard him whisper the first word of the Hebrew blessing for the Sabbath and they realized that his request was tied to his spirituality. She said, "When I look at my son, I think, 'He's not broken. He's just neurologically outnumbered, like me.'"

On her Facebook page in August 2022, autistic actress, social media personality, disability rights activist, and author Chloé Hayden wrote:

> For my entire life, I've been told to "quiet my autism," to downplay my natural instincts in how I cope, react and move in the world around me in order to appease, appeal and comfort its mainly neurotypical inhabitants.
>
> I was constantly met with "talk with your mouth, not your hands," while doing oral presentations at school.
>
> And "if you weren't so . . . autistic, we'd be happy to give you the job," by casting agents.
>
> And "hey, can you not do that thing with your hands? It makes you look like a weirdo and I don't want people thinking I'm weird too," from my friends.
>
> It was acting teachers, agents and industry professionals telling me if I wanted to find my place in the entertainment industry, I needed to act more neurotypical.
>
> So, anyway, here's a photo of me stimming after closing Australian Fashion Week's first ever Adaptive Runway.
>
> I do not exist to make neurotypicals comfortable.

Many accounts given by disabled people reference the pain and frustration related to constantly being told that you are broken. A post on the Facebook page Disabled in Massachusetts from December 2022 summed up Disability as a Deficit from the perspective of disabled people so succinctly: "Ableds have a lot of nerve telling disabled folks to 'overcome adversity' especially when they are the adversity."

It seems that nondisabled people who view Disability as a Deficit often assume that disabled people also view their disabilities as deficits. Though that is true for some, it is not true for all. In her memoir *Easy Beauty*, Chloé Cooper Jones writes:

> The term "disability" did not help me understand myself but was instead a tool for deciphering strange and disorienting moments when strangers would look at me and decide who I was and what I could do. People saw contrast between their bodies and mine. They saw absence, lack. But I, having only ever been in my body, did not feel lacking. Going up the stairs feels like going up the stairs. Walking feels like walking. It looks strange, I guess, to those who watch me. It looks lesser. But I had no reason to feel lesser.

In *I Will Die on this Hill* by Meghan Ashburn and Jules Edwards, Edwards writes:

> As a child, I was an eloper, mess-maker, nudist with sensory difficulties. I had an affinity for water and stair cartwheels and an inability to pronounce even my own name. My family jokingly gave me two Indian names—"Little Naked Running Girl" and "Crash Boom Bang Fall Down the Stairs."
>
> Today, I'm a late-diagnosed autistic and ADHD mother of three Black and Ojibwe autistic children, one diagnosed at each pseudo "level" of autism. I am a community builder. I've

been the first person that people have asked, "Am I autistic?" I've been the first person that parents of autistic children have asked, "What do I do?" I am a complex and whole human being. I am autistic, and I'm not missing a piece.

In *Disability Visibility*, an anthology of personal essays edited by Alice Wong, Jessica Slice writes about her experience as a disabled parent. Jessica has Ehlers-Danlos syndrome, which causes a range of symptoms that can present inconsistently. She vulnerably shares the complex feelings that come with her personal circumstances. She writes about how her disability sometimes limits her ability to perform some tasks of parenting but also highlights the ways her disability has enhanced her parenting.

> Many new moms resent that period of being stuck indoors, but I loved it: I spend most of my time at home or in bed, and Khalil brought tremendous joy and purpose to those hours. My physical capacities matched his emotional and physical demands beautifully. He was a happy baby, as long as we were touching, and cuddling him for most of every day was an easy need to meet. To this day, whenever he's away from me, I feel a longing right on my sternum. It aches a little and feels too light.

Later in the chapter, she adds:

> I like to imagine that, soon, he will find comfort in the fact that I am so often around, steady and patient, ready to listen. Years of restricted movement have trained me to attend, to slow down, to savor. Parenting is a series of phases; as we both grow and change, there will be new intersections between the needs of his body and the needs of mine.

When we view Disability as a Deficit, it prevents us from recognizing the beauty that exists within people with disabilities.

What Does This Look Like in Action? Manifestations of Disability as a Deficit

1. Putting yourself in their shoes

Disability as a Deficit sometimes manifests through people's attempts at putting themselves in the disabled person's shoes to try to process the ways that their physical disability would presumably change the way they sense and/or move through the world. Though empathy is an important part of our humanity, we can't ever fully understand an experience that we have not endured. It's "putting yourself in their shoes" when you have only ever worn tennis shoes and they wear wooden clogs and you assume the shoes are comparable. When a disability results in a person not having access to a specific sense or skill that the majority of people do have access to, it leads to people pondering what it would be like to function without it. The pondering person knows how much they rely on that sense or skill, which often leads them to presuming that being without it would put them at a disadvantage. What we aren't factoring in, however, is that most disabled people didn't become disabled yesterday. Some were born with a disability and have never experienced a loss of a particular sense or skill set. When we make these presumptions, we forget that disabled people eventually get used to their disability and find their way to accommodations and supports that can help them be successful in different ways. This is why simulation activities can be problematic and nonrepresentative. A sighted person putting on a blindfold will not create the same experience as a blind person. It might lead to insight regarding what types of activities would need to be done differently, but the feelings generated during these kinds of activities usually do not align with the experiences of those from the community whose experience they are trying to simulate. There is a place for these activities, but the nuances and caveats need to be explicitly discussed.

Being Dan's mom has shown me how many people assume that not having vision creates major disadvantages for a person. As a person who has always been sighted, I used to hold the same misconception. When I started working with blind and visually impaired children, and eventually when I became Dan's mom, it became clear that blindness is not a deficit. Dan's blindness is a nonissue when he is not disadvantaged by lack of access or accommodation. At home, Dan has everything that he needs to access his environment. At school, he is learning braille and reads the same content that his classmates are reading, because his support staff make sure that his copies are brailled. He works with a teacher of the visually impaired daily who teaches him not only braille but also math structures as well as how to use accessibility features with technology, such as voice-over on an iPad. He has access to orientation and mobility teaching to help him learn to use his long white cane along with various landmarks and strategies to travel in a world that was not designed with blind people in mind. At home, we use audio descriptions, when it is an option, so that he can enjoy shows and movies.

With accessibility and accommodation, there isn't anything that he cannot participate in or accomplish because of his blindness. So if someone were to ask him, "What is wrong with you?" the answer would be "nothing."

The same is true for other disabilities that involve differences in the way a body functions. When a person is seen using a long white cane, sign language, a wheelchair, or a prosthesis, there is often an automatic assumption that something is "wrong" with the person.

Challenge Yourself

Instead of viewing disability through the lens of what you think your life would be like if you were in the position of the disabled person, try to reframe your thinking to include what the disabled person's life is like with, and without, accommodations and access. For example, if you are a hearing person, it might be scary to think of what it would be like to suddenly lose your hearing. There is validity in assuming that losing a sense abruptly would be scary and sad, and many people who have experienced just that have reported that to be their truth. Most Deaf people didn't lose their hearing yesterday, though, and with supports in place, they aren't missing access to life or the experiences that make life beautiful. (This doesn't mean that the person's feelings about their disability aren't important, and we will talk more about that later.)

If the topic of disability comes up and your child is processing disability in this same way, you can empower her to avoid the pitfall of assigning deficit by talking explicitly about the importance of accommodation and accessibility. For example, if your child said something like "He can't hear? That means he can't even watch movies!" this gives you a chance to respond with information about how d/Deaf people access auditory information from movies. "Actually, d/Deaf people can use something called closed captioning to get the information that we hear with our ears. I'll turn on closed captioning when we get home so that you can see what it's like." You can go on to talk about how frustrating it must be for d/Deaf people when they do not have access to closed captions, and how it can lead to being left out, which will allow for your child to process the importance of access.

2. Ostracizing aspects of disability that are outside a predetermined norm

Many people with visible disabilities are ostracized for their equipment and physical difference. Differences in a person's neurology and how their brain processes information can be viewed as a deficit as well, simply because they are not the same as everyone else's. Often, the barriers that disabled people are up against are the result of cultural standards that dictate what ways of existing are considered "normal." What has been accepted as "normal" has been built into the foundations of systems we are often mandated to participate in, including educational, social, and vocational. Put simply, what we have defined as normal has become the mold that people are expected to fit into. There are many examples that fall into this manifestation, and the following list is nonexhaustive.

People with disabilities have reported feeling ostracized for existing in ways outside of the box that include:

- Having intense focus on one particular subject matter
- Talking a lot or talking fast
- Being very quiet and viewed as disconnected
- Reading with reduced fluency or mispronouncing words
- Requiring a lot of rest or fatiguing easily
- Demonstrating preference for, or adherence to, ritual and routine
- Having motor or verbal tics
- Communicating in ways other than mouth speaking
- Moving body parts in unique and/or repetitive ways
- Having a lower-than-average IQ
- Avoiding eye contact
- Daydreaming

The things that people are ostracized for usually are what feel most natural for them and sometimes serve an important purpose. During his 2020 TED Talk called "What It's Really Like to Have Autism," Ethan Lisi talks about the reasons behind some of the things that autistic people get ostracized for.

> Think about all of the social gatherings you've been to in the past. Was there loud music playing? Were there really bright lights? Were there lots of different food smells going on at the same time? Were there lots of conversations happening all at once? Those things may not have bothered you guys, but for someone with autism, they can be quite overwhelming. So in those situations, we do something called stimming, which is like a repetitive motion or a noise or some other random fidgeting that may or may not seem normal. Some people will flap their arms or make a noise or spin. Yeah, it's basically our way of zoning out. It can often feel necessary for us to stim. However, it's often frowned upon and we're forced to hide it.

Challenge Yourself

Try shifting your thinking to a place of openness to the vastness of the human condition. Many people are ostracized for attributes that cause no harm to others and have been exiled to the fringe based on societal bias and stigma. If your child asks you, "Why does that person [insert observable difference here]?" consider keeping your answer simple and factual. Stick to what you know or can assume with the information you have. Answers like "Because that is what works best for them" or "Because that is what they do" meet that criteria. You can add things like "We are all made differently" or "We all do things differently," and you can even throw in a side of "It's OK if people do things differently than you do. Wouldn't it be boring if we were all the same?" Trying to speculate a more specific answer to the *why* will often get you into trouble, unless your child is asking you about a person you know on a very personal level.

You can also offer examples specific to your family to help your child make connections and associations that might reinforce the concept, but stay within the bounds of your expertise as someone who knows the details. "Your hair is brown and your brother's is blond." "Some kids in your class wear glasses and others don't." "You talk faster and louder than your sibling, who tends to talk slower and more quietly." "Your dad likes to read books, but I like to listen to books instead." "Your sister loves to be with big groups of other kids, but you prefer to hang out with one or two close friends." "When you get worried, you start asking more questions, but when your sibling gets worried, they get very quiet."

3. Being closed off to the gifts that disability can offer

When people view Disability as a Deficit, they are unable to see the gifts that disabled people bring to the world. (And, if you think the gift is in the ways they inspire us, go back and reread chapter 2.) Harvey Blume was the first person to use the term *neurodiversity*, in his article in the *Atlantic* in 1998, "Neurodiversity: On the Neurological Underpinnings of Geekdom." He wrote, "Neurodiversity may be every bit as crucial for the human race as biodiversity is for life in general. Who can say what form of wiring will prove best at any given moment?"

In *NeuroTribes*, the social and behavioral intricacies of the men who have been coined the "fathers of physics," Henry Cavendish and Paul Dirac, are outlined. They demonstrated absolute scientific brilliance and created social bewilderment for those who knew them. Silberman writes:

> It's hard to imagine the state of the modern world if these
> two remarkable scientists had never lived. Many aspects of

life that we currently take for granted might never have been invented. Both men may have wondered at times if they had accidentally been born on the wrong planet, among chatty, well-intentioned creatures who wasted precious time trying to impress, flatter, outwit, and seduce each other. But their atypical minds were uncannily suited to the work they were born to do. They lived their lives in ways that were as precise, ritualized, and methodical as their experiments.

Disability as a Deficit keeps us from recognizing that a person's disability can give them strengths and perspectives that those not experiencing life the way they do won't have.

Challenge Yourself

Remember that humanity is complex, and each human has strengths and challenges. Disabled people are no exception. My kids and I constantly talk about how each one of us is unique and has something to offer that is different from everyone else. Make this an ongoing conversation with your kids, going out of your way to talk about what they are good at, what their siblings are good at, what their parents are good at, and so on. They will have the chance to think about how each person's individuality lends to their strengths, which will be beneficial in future interactions with others, both disabled and nondisabled.

4. Intellectual elitism and the "grammar police"

I am a good speller and used to take great pleasure in showing off my spelling and grammar prowess, sometimes unfortunately by laughing about misspellings and grammatical errors made by others. I felt and demonstrated an abundance of smugness and needed life to throw some water in my face.

When Pete was diagnosed as dyslexic and I started to learn more about it, I began to feel very different about my former position on the grammar pedestal. It started to feel gross up there. I realized how ableist it is to mock others for things like academic performance.

After I started learning more about dyslexia, I started to wonder if it was possible that my dad is dyslexic. I remembered him mentioning things about reading and writing when I was a kid, but we had never had a specific conversation about it before. On a recent trip home to Kansas, we had a talk about it, and he shared experiences with me that led me to believe that he probably is. I showed him a spoken-word poem by R. J. Wright called "Dyslexia" on YouTube. R. J. shares about the ways that he has been shamed for his challenges with reading, writing, and spelling:

> . . . so the first girl that I ever wrote a love letter to told me
> "you write like a toddler"
> She laughed as she read every spelling and grammar mistake
> to a chorus of cackling schoolgirls.
> And ever since that day
> I haven't been able to unwrite the reflection
> —I mean the rejection—I mean
> I have dyslexia.
> A disorder that involves difficulty learning to read and write
> and I hate telling people because of the way
> that you're looking at me
> right now.

My dad was moved by the poetry. It seemed as if he felt seen, after over sixty years of wondering why reading and writing were so much harder for him. My dad didn't finish high school, and I could see that weighed on him throughout his life. He has frequently commented over the years that he didn't know how he ended up with kids who are so smart. My dad planned and constructed his two-story shop and most of the childhood home that I go back to in Kansas. He is an inventor of several machines that make his life easier, and I swear he can fix anything. Because of the way we treat people who misspell words, struggle to read, and drop out of school, though, my dad spent much of his life feeling as if something were wrong with him. He is another part of where my passion to write this book comes from.

My dad strongly connected with the portions of Wright's poetry that spoke to misspelled words and improper grammar being made fun of on social media. He specifically connected with a part of the poem that addressed the many versions of *there/their/they're*.

As I mentioned before, I used to be a person who did this. Now when I see people being mocked for spelling or grammar, I picture the dejected faces of a couple of guys I love very dearly. And it punches me right in the heart.

Challenge Yourself

When someone misspells a word or makes grammatical mistakes, usually their meaning is still easy to determine. If you are the person's teacher, professor, or supervisor and their spelling or grammar doesn't meet your expectations, it seems appropriate to connect with the person to see if they need resources or accommodations to support their ability to complete assignments to your expectation. If you are not in a teacher or supervisor position, though, you really don't need to point out someone's mistake.

If you can't understand what the person means, you can ask them for clarification in a respectful way that doesn't demean them. While you're at it, try to avoid intellectual elitism in general. It's pretty much always ableist. I have seen people online suggest that if the person who makes vocabulary, grammar, or spelling errors is being nasty or unkind, then it is OK to demean them. I disagree. In my opinion, ableism is unacceptable regardless of the situation. Excusing yourself for ableism because you don't like a person seems to me to be another manifestation of ableism. Of course, you get to decide what is right for you, but if you are looking to avoid perpetuating ableism, my advice is to turn in your grammar police badge. There are many other ways to save the world that might be more fruitful.

5. Framing disability barriers appropriately

In a June 2021 *Forbes* article, "Fighting Ableism Is About Much More than Attitudes and Awareness," journalist Andrew Pulrang wrote:

> The disability community has long understood that there are really *two* main kinds of ableism. First, there are personal prejudices, misconceptions and reactions that individuals have about disabled people. Then there are the less personal, but more concrete and materially harmful examples of ableism that are baked into our physical environment, as well as our laws, policies, and everyday practices.

When we attribute challenges that disabled people face to their disability, equipment, or aids, we are guilty of another manifestation of Disability as a Deficit by reinforcing the laws, policies, and everyday practices that lead to access barriers. It is important to remember that it is not the disability that is problematic but rather the lack of access and accommodations.

When we say things like "He can't get into the building because of his wheelchair," it suggests that the wheelchair is the problem when, in reality, the building's limited access options are the problem—he can't get into the building because it has no ramp. When we say, "I'm sorry, ma'am, but if you are d/Deaf you won't be able to hear the actors in the play," the barrier is not a person's hearing status but rather that the only way to access the show's dialogue is through hearing. The accessibility failure, in this case, would be the lack of sign language interpreters or closed-captioning options.

How we frame the barriers that negatively affect disabled people is a very important part of dismantling ableism. The systems that perpetuate ongoing access barriers have no reason to change if we never hold them accountable for the barriers they create. If we are to make an inclusive society, the idea that access doesn't have to be universal needs to be one that we outgrow.

Challenge Yourself

Be mindful of how you talk about disability and access barriers. Practice reframing examples of access, or lack thereof, by centering access instead of centering someone's disability. When you notice a person's disability being identified as the problem in a situation, speak up. With your kids, practice using language that centers access. "This menu isn't accessible, so people who are blind can't use it. I wonder if this restaurant has a brailled menu." "This building has a ramp, so it is accessible to everyone." "Let's make a voice recording of the information from the invitation to send to your friend who doesn't read print so that she can access it."

Modeling an expectation of access, and an effort to meet that expectation, will help your kids grow up understanding that access for all is a goal worthy of expecting and striving for.

6. One-sided blame and the "double empathy problem"

The double empathy problem is a theory that is decades old; autistic researcher Damian Milton coined the term in 2012. The double empathy problem theory posits that communication breakdowns between autistic and nonautistic—sometimes referred to as *allistic*—people are caused by *both* parties' difficulties understanding each other.

What we understand about autism has been changing and evolving since 1943, when the behavioral profile was first proposed by Leo Kanner. Since the neurotype's diagnostic inception, however, the prominent belief has been that social communication in autistic individuals is in deficit, and treatment for social communication has rested on the foundation that autistic people are to blame for communication breakdowns in social interactions with allistics.

Autistic adults, however, have been sharing the harmful effects this foundational belief has had on them and have offered their own experiences as a way to understand why this way of looking at social challenges is faulty. Some have used the analogy of different operating systems, such as iOS versus Android: different but not right or wrong. Many graphics have been created to help people understand this concept, but my personal favorite was created by a content creator for the page NeuroWild. This popular illustration explains the double empathy problem through the analogy of squirrels and beavers. Squirrels can communicate with other squirrels fine, and beavers communicate with other beavers fine, and this graphic proposes the question: When miscommunication between squirrels and beavers takes place, who carries the burden of repair? It goes on to note that society has decided it is the responsibility of squirrels to fix the problem and asks if that seems appropriate. It then makes the connection to communication breakdowns between autistic and nonautistic people, suggesting that the proper way to address these miscommunications is to teach all kids that communication is a two-way street and that learning about the ways others communicate is important.

Researchers at the University of Texas at Dallas conducted research examining the influence of specific factors on the perceived quality of social interaction among participants. The study and results were summarized in a January 2020 article by Stephen Fontenot titled "Study Challenges Assumptions About Social Interaction Difficulties in Autism." A total of 125 adults held short, unstructured conversations with an unfamiliar person. About half of those participants, sixty-seven total, were autistic. Afterward, each participant evaluated the quality of the interaction. Dr. Noah Sasson, an associate professor in the School of Behavioral and Brain Sciences and corresponding author of the study, summarized the results.

> These findings suggest that social interaction difficulties in autism are not an absolute characteristic of the individual. Rather, social quality is a relational characteristic that depends upon the fit between the person and the social environment. If autistic people were inherently poor at social interaction, you'd expect an interaction between two autistic people to be even more of a struggle than between an autistic and non-autistic person. But that's not what we found.

The study found that both groups, autistic and nonautistic, reported preference for future interaction to be with their specific neurotype. Autistic participants reported disclosing more and feeling closer to autistic conversation partners than nonautistic partners.

The term *neurokin* is often used in neurodivergent spaces and refers to a person or people who are the same neurotype. Many in the neurodivergent community have shared the profound importance of neurokin in one's life. Kristy Forbes, a neurodivergent parent, advocate, and educator, wrote a beautiful post about neurokin in March 2021 on her Facebook page Autism & ND Support.

> In my work, I promote positive autistic identity. I am heavily immersed in a beautiful autistic community that is made up of people from all over the world—varying in ages, genders, sexualities, races and creeds. Many of us know an autistic person when we see one. But it's never about their

knowledge, IQ, academic achievements or challenges, their fine and gross motor skills or their social and communicative differences. It's their energy. It's a beautiful, powerful recognition of our own. Our neurokin. It is an unspoken language. There is no shame in being autistic.

Challenge Yourself

It might seem that social norms are so ingrained that they seem impossible to compromise, but the pandemic that started in 2020 showed us that we can adapt. We learned we can do things differently and still find ways to connect and meet goals.

One way to help your children understand that communication is a two-way street, and that there isn't one correct way to communicate, socialize, interact, or *exist*, is to be explicit in teaching them about differing viewpoints and styles. When you and your child have a disagreement or misunderstanding, taking the time to talk about what you and your child were each thinking about and feeling separately, and acknowledging both as valid, is a great way to teach your child to consider how individual differences can influence an interaction. These lessons don't have to be specific to disability and will be helpful in interactions with people who vary in a number of ways.

For example, "When I said, 'No more candy,' you got really upset because you thought I meant you could never have candy again. What I meant was that you cannot have candy right now, but I didn't say that. My brain decided you knew what I meant, but I was wrong. Next time, I will say, 'No more candy until,' and I will tell you when you can have candy again, so that you will have the information that you need. If I forget, you can always ask me, 'When can I have candy again?'" This example identifies how the communication breakdown happened and helps a child understand how someone else's thoughts can be different from theirs and how those differences can affect an

interaction. If you interact with a person who communicates differently and your child asks questions, you can connect these examples.
"Remember that time that you and I had different ideas about how
to talk about the candy? People communicate about things in lots of
different ways."

In addition, it is beneficial to take inventory of the "shoulds"
that you hold and that most likely steer the ways you influence your
children to socially interact with others. Many of us have opinions
about things like eye contact, handshakes, and other social customs.
If you hold the belief that it is important to look at someone's face
when talking to them, and then interact with someone who doesn't
maintain eye contact, you are likely to hold beliefs about them that
may or may not be true. Because communication styles can vary, be
aware of what you teach your children as fact and be open to expand-
ing your understanding of the different ways that people socialize.

Bring It Home

Pay attention to which differences you point out to your children. If
you find yourself pointing out a difference, look inside and ask yourself
why you feel compelled by that particular difference. Is your intent
to educate your kids to promote understanding and acceptance? Is it
to promote caution? Certainly, there will be a variety of reasons that
can all be warranted, depending on what you are discussing with
them, but looking at *why* will help you understand potential biases
that exist in you. For example, if you find yourself pointing out/jok-
ing when people misspell words, consider why spelling is important
to you and what you may have been taught or conditioned to think
about it. Go a step further and think about the reasons why someone
might misspell words. Is it because of a lack of education? How do
you view people you assume are uneducated? How do you want your
children to think about others in relation to how educated they are?

Do people misspell because of an intellectual disability or learning disability? What are your personal feelings about intellectual disability and learning disability? Is stigma at play? Do you want your children to assign explanations that may or may not be true to the situation, or would you prefer that they consider the ability to spell might depend on a variety of factors? Leaning into the idea that humans are complex and that variations and differences aren't anything to be afraid of, and modeling that outlook, will influence how your children react to differences that they see in others.

In the book *Just Right for You: A Story About Autism*, author Melanie Heyworth highlights how the ways a person exists in the world are representative of what is right for them. It is a book written for an autistic child but includes insight that would also be beneficial for nonautistic children to consider. She writes:

> From the moment you began to grow, I knew that you would be just right.
>
> No matter what you looked like, or what things you enjoyed, or what made you laugh, I knew that you would be just right.
>
> No matter what you found hard, or what things you disliked, or what made you cry, I knew that you would be just right.
>
> From the moment you began to grow, I also knew your brain would be just right.
>
> Not right for someone else.
>
> But just right, just for you.

Empowering your children to understand individuality as a beautiful part of themselves will help enable them to see individuality as a beautiful part of others.

4

"THAT'S SO SAD"

DISABILITY AS A TRAGEDY

I N HER MEMOIR *Just Human*, Arielle Silverman writes:

> Yet, I learned from a young age that blindness bothers many
> other people. I have heard of blindness described as a trag-
> edy, a curse, a devastation, or a prison sentence. In popula-
> tion surveys, blindness is rated as one of the most feared
> "diseases" surpassed only by cancer and AIDS. Much of my
> life has been spent on trying to understand how a condition
> that feels so normal and inconsequential to me would be so
> upsetting to outside observers.

Disability as a Tragedy tells us the lie that disability is a terrible
misfortune, regardless of individual circumstances. People who perpetuate this form of ableism often think that what they are offering
is compassion, but in reality, it's pity. In *Bringing Home the Dharma*,
Jack Kornfield writes:

> The near enemy of compassion is pity. Instead of feeling the
> openness of compassion, pity says, "Oh, that poor person.
> I feel sorry for people like that." Pity sees them different
> from ourselves. It sets up a separation between ourselves
> and others, a sense of distance and remoteness from the
> suffering of others that is affirming and gratifying to the self.

There certainly are aspects of a person's circumstances that war-
rant compassion, but those are specific to each person and are con-
tingent on whether the person considers their circumstances to be a
hardship. Have you ever been on the receiving end of pity or sympathy
for something you didn't feel bad about? It feels awful. People tell me
that it must be so hard to have a disabled child, with pity in their
faces, and it is very discouraging. I understand that people assume
they are being empathetic and compassionate, but they are making
decisions for me about the way I feel that I do not agree with. They
are implying truths that are not true for me. I understand that some
parents of disabled children might feel bad about their situation, but
the overarching assumption that all parents must feel that way is the
problem.

In 1993, the Autism Network International newsletter, *Our Voice*,
shared a letter by Jim Sinclair titled "Don't Mourn for Us" that was
originally to be given to parents of autistic individuals. The letter was
based on a presentation he gave at the 1993 International Conference
on Autism in Toronto.

> This is what I think autism societies should be about: not
> mourning for what never was, but exploration of what is.
> We need you. We need your help and your understanding.
> Your world is not very open to us, and we won't make it
> without your strong support. Yes, there is tragedy that comes
> with autism: not because of what we are, but because of the

things that happen to us. Be sad about that, if you want to be sad about something. Better than being sad about it, though, get mad about it—and then *do* something about it. The tragedy is not that we're here, but that your world has no place for us to be. How can it be otherwise, as long as our own parents are still grieving over having brought us into the world?

Disability as a Tragedy can be a source of shame and insecurity for people with disabilities. In his book *Have Dog, Will Travel*, Stephen Kuusisto tells of his experiences with blindness and the beautiful personal journey he endeavored with his first guide dog. He writes:

> Disability has numerous implications. One can live a long while recognizing only some of them. In the 1950s my parents couldn't imagine a future for me if I presented as blind. They forcefully encouraged me to do absolutely everything sighted children did, minus any acknowledgment of my difference.

At the age of thirty-eight, when he learned to use a white cane while preparing to be paired with a guide dog, he describes how he felt walking in public for the first time with a white cane.

> I was so self-conscious my skin felt tight. It was my mother. She was telling me to avoid being blind. She was saying it was shameful. Even though I was listening to [orientation and mobility teacher] Mike I was worried about strangers. Did they see me from their front windows? Were people whispering about me? I imagined someone saying: "Look at that man with his white stick, how sad!"

Rarely is pity appreciated or received as helpful. Even when people have complex feelings about their disability and wish they were not disabled, being pitied is still often unwelcome.

Disability as a Tragedy also shows up when a disabled child is born. Karen Ryan is an advocate and mother to Violet, who has Down syndrome. In an interview for Special Olympics Game Changers on ESPN's website, Karen talks about the day Violet was born.

> When she was born, there was no "congratulations," there was no, like, "Your baby is beautiful and happy and she's alive" and you know, all that. It was just, "It looks like she has Down syndrome."

She goes on to say:

> I wish I wouldn't have cried when she was born, but it's just 'cause you don't know and you're just afraid of what you don't know. But I haven't stopped enjoying it since then, and it's been kind of my mission, that no mom cries like I cried when Violet was born.

It is also sometimes considered a tragedy when a disabled person announces that they will soon become a parent. The blogger Alex Dacy, who goes by Wheelchair Rapunzel, explains the way she was treated when she announced that she was pregnant. She shares a comment that was made on her announcement: "You are not capable of doing this. I'm in no way disabled and raising my children is hard. You—quite literally—are in no form . . . capable. This is so selfish and pitiful."

A disabled person being told they are incapable and selfish for becoming a parent is blatant ableism, as is the implication that disabled people cannot be good parents.

Disability as a Tragedy also cultivates the misconception that disabled people aren't lovable. In a November 2022 Facebook post on the page Hazelwood Consulting, Rachel Hazelwood shared the following:

They say
You're so lucky they love you
Disability and all
You're so lucky to have them
Even though you are . . . like that

I say
I am not a flaw
My body and mind deserve to be cherished
Not despite
Not even though
But because they are mine

What Does This Look Like in Action? Manifestations of Disability as a Tragedy

1. Automatic responses of sadness or pity when disability is discovered or disclosed

I have lost count of the number of times I have told someone Dan is blind and the response I get is a sad face or some embodiment of sorrow or pity.

I don't find a difference between adults and children in terms of the frequency of pity responses, but there is a difference in how they respond. Because of children's nature, they are often direct and uninhibited and usually verbally express sadness rather than just subtly changing their affect or making a sad facial expression. I do not fault them, because they only know what they have been told or have absorbed from their culture. On one occasion a child asked if Dan was blind, and when I answered yes, she said, "Oh, that's so sad," expressing genuine sadness on her face and through her body. I responded that we don't think it's sad at all and went on to share a few quick notes of education and advocacy.

On one shining occasion, a child we met at the playground listened as Dan answered his question about why he uses a cane, and he responded with "That's pretty cool." That had never happened before, and it was incredibly refreshing. Dan and the boy went on to interact as children often do without Dan or I having to clear up the false black cloud that almost always makes its way into his interactions. That interaction gave me hope for the future.

Challenge Yourself

Take the time to confront your own feelings about disability. If you find yourself reacting with sadness, or what you perceive to be compassion, dig into those feelings. Is it because the person seems to be suffering in some way? Or is it because you have determined that suffering is an automatic part of disability? Making this distinction will help you reframe the way that you view, and react to, disability. This will be important for children in your care, because they are always watching your reactions. If they see you reacting with sadness, they will internalize that disability is something to be sad about. If you accept disability as a normal part of the human condition and don't react, they will more likely internalize that disability alone might elicit a notice but doesn't need a reaction. This probably doesn't need to be said after what I just wrote, but I will say it anyway. Don't tell someone you feel sad about their disability unless they have told you they feel sad about their disability. Many disabled people don't feel sad about their disability, so you shouldn't either.

2. Expressing sorrow instead of joy in disability pregnancy and birth announcements

Disability as a Tragedy often shows up when a child who is born, or soon to be born, is announced to have a disability. How a parent feels about their child's disability is personal and complex, but ableism is in full view when friends and acquaintances share anything other than the excitement that is standard when a nondisabled baby is announced to the world.

Parents will have complex feelings about having a disabled child. Those complex feelings are often the result of ableism and fears related to how the world will view and treat their child. Imagine what an impact it would make if the default sentiment was "Congratulations!" rather than "I'm sorry." If the world celebrated disabled newborns the same way that it celebrates nondisabled newborns, some of those parental fears would be alleviated.

Challenge Yourself

This one is easy. Offering congratulations is the appropriate response when someone is announcing a pregnancy or the arrival of a child. Congratulating parents, or being happy for them, will not invalidate the complex feelings they might be having and, rather, will send the message that their child is celebrated and accepted. If you view these announcements with anything less than the excitement you feel when disability is not part of an announcement, do the personal work that you need to do to confront your ableism and refrain from responding with sentiments that might cast a shadow.

As I noted, it is understandable for a parent to worry that their disabled child will not be accepted. Keep in mind that when people share sentiments of sorrow in response to the arrival of a disabled child, they are applying the very mistreatment that parents of disabled children are often afraid of. If the world feels sorry for me because this is how my child is, what are the chances my child will be accepted and embraced?

Similar to the danger of making assumptions about how a person feels about their disability, it is also important to not assume how a parent will feel about becoming a parent to a disabled child. Parents will share intimate feelings with close confidants, and the rest of us should avoid making assumptions.

3. Conveying that disabled people are lucky to be loved

When people find out that we adopted Dan, they usually ask if we knew he was blind before we decided to adopt him. People often seem surprised when I tell them we did indeed know ahead of time. This is a glaring example of Disability as a Tragedy. The underlying implication is that people wouldn't choose to have a disabled child in their family. This saddens me greatly, because I know that one day Dan will undoubtedly feel the pain of sharing his story with someone and having them respond with shock or surprise at the idea that his parents would choose him given that he is disabled. I wish I could shield him from this, but I know it is inevitable, so we have to make sure that he feels secure in who he is, so he is equipped to see able-ism for what it is.

Challenge Yourself

Recognize that it is hurtful to imply that someone is lucky to be loved, regardless of the circumstances, and never tell a disabled person that they are lucky to have friends or family members who stand by them despite their disability. Also remember that it isn't a noble act to choose to love someone with a disability.

4. Differing views on the death of disabled people

A 2008 Reuters article by Claire Sibonney shared results from an online poll commissioned by Disaboom. The poll revealed that 52 percent of the one thousand Americans polled, who were described as "nationally represented," reported they would rather die than suffer a severe disability.

The ways that disabled people are affected seem to be judged by the general public to be so tragic that you also see this manifest when disabled people die. Comments are often made about how people with physical disabilities are probably now running in heaven, and the blind can now see and the d/Deaf can now hear.

In her book *Say Hello*, Carly Findlay discusses how people talk about death differently when it is the death of a disabled person. An example she gives that aligns with her disability is people saying things like "Everyone's skin is perfect in heaven." She asks, "How can a child be confident when they're told their best life will be when they're dead?"

Unless I missed it, I have never heard this type of talk in a non-disabled person's eulogy. It isn't common to talk about the things that a person could not do in life; rather, eulogies usually seem to highlight what a person was good at. If it were common to eulogize people with the barriers they faced, my eulogy might include something like "Carrie is free now, probably sticking to a daily exercise routine in heaven, and remembering tasks and appointments without setting any alarms or timers."

In all seriousness, the only exception that comes to mind is talk of being free from suffering when eulogizing someone whose illness dramatically affected their quality of life. End-of-life suffering should not be compared to long-term disabilities. When disability includes pain and suffering, compassion makes sense. An assumption that a person was suffering simply because he or she was disabled, however, is ableist.

Challenge Yourself

Those who were close to a recently deceased disabled person will be privy to personal information that is true for that person and might be included in a tribute to their life. Strangers who are unfamiliar with how a person felt about their disability, though, should avoid statements that cast the disability in a negative light when talking about the disabled person's death. Sharing typical condolences is sufficient and will help steer you away from accidental ableism.

5. Withholding vulnerability in friendship because of assumed burdens

Disability as a Tragedy is also responsible when people withhold vulnerability from a friend because the friend is disabled. On the *Crutches and Spice* podcast, hosted by disabled activist Imani Barbarin, Imani and her boyfriend Tito Quevedo talk about this manifestation during an episode from December 2019. Tito talks about how his friends often refrain from sharing their struggles with him because of his disability: "He's on dialysis so let me never come to him with a problem ever."

Imani adds, "It makes you feel like a litmus test for their problem. It's like, no, everyone is entitled to their problems."

Authentic, healthy friendship is a two-way interaction. When one side of the friendship has determined that the other side isn't capable of holding up their end of the deal, regardless of the reason, it skews the friendship into a different type of relationship. Disabled people deserve authentic friendships that include mutual trust, and it isn't fair to deny them that authenticity because of assumptions rooted in ableism.

Challenge Yourself

Though your intentions might be good when withholding struggles from a disabled friend, your impact will be to the detriment of your friendship. I suspect most people do this because they assume disabled people are already overwhelmed or weighed down by their own hardships. Remember, though, many disabled people don't consider their disability to be a hardship. Others might have once considered aspects of their disability to be a hardship but are now more accustomed to, and accepting of, them. If you are unsure, you can ask your friend, "Are you up for me venting to you about a few things that I'm struggling with?" If the friend is truly overwhelmed by their personal circumstances, this gives them the option to decline but shows them that you do indeed trust them with your struggles and reject the idea that their disability is a tragedy that prevents them from being a good friend.

Bring It Home

Share resources that normalize disability with the children in your care so they have the opportunity to see disability as an ordinary part of the human condition and not anything tragic. By adding books to your library with stories about disabled people participating in typical activities, you negate any potential tragedy with normalcy. *Dad and Me in the Morning* by Patricia Lakin is a beautiful children's story about a d/Deaf boy and his dad waking up early to watch the sunrise together. The book never explicitly references d/Deafness or hearing loss but mentions a flashing alarm clock, hearing aids, lipreading, and how the boy can feel his dad walking down the stairs. What makes this story extraordinary is that it weaves in disability without making it the focal point or injecting tragedy or inspiration.

5

"CAN I PRAY FOR YOU?"

DISABILITY AS SOMETHING TO BE CURED

I F DISABILITY AS A TRAGEDY tells us that to be disabled is sad, Disability as Something to Be Cured goes one step further and tells us that a disabled person would be better if they were cured—and that every disabled person wishes to be cured.

In the book *Disability Visibility*, Liz Moore states:

> There is a persistent belief amongst abled people that a cure is what disabled people should want. To abandon our disabled bodies and selves and assimilate it into perhaps an unachievable abled skin. Pushback to this idea often comes in the form of the social model of disability, which states that we are disabled by society and a lack of access rather than by our bodies.

It seems to be a very common misconception that all disabled people desire to be "cured." It is true that some disabled people do

71

wish for a cure, but that is not true for everyone. The assumption that everyone wishes for a cure is a source of ableism.

In a video on the BBC Three YouTube channel called "Things People with Down Syndrome Are Tired of Hearing," adults with Down syndrome answer questions and respond to common misconceptions about their condition. When asked, "Do you wish you didn't have Down syndrome?" participants gave the following answers:

> No. Why? It's just me. It's part of me.
> I may have Down syndrome, but without it, I don't think
>   I'd really be me.
> I don't wish that. I wish that people would see Down syndrome
>   in a positive light.
> My motto in life is: Down syndrome? So what?

We must remember that this form of ableism sometimes takes its toll on disabled people through the shame that comes from the suggestion that they would be better if they weren't disabled. Feelings of being a burden, combined with feelings about how happy their loved one(s) would be if they were no longer disabled, add layers of complexity.

The following excerpt is from the young adult adaption of *Disability Visibility* and was written by June Eric-Udorie.

> A deacon handed me a little plastic cup containing fruit wine. On top was a thin wafer of bread, the sign of the cross imprinted in the middle. "Dip the bread in the wine and place the communion on your eyes," my grandmother said. "If you *really* believe, if you really pray and cry out, then God will heal you."
>
> I sighed, took a deep breath as my insides coiled from shame, and did as I was told. The words came out as a

breathy whisper: *"Pretty women wonder where my secret lies."* Maya Angelou comforted me as I placed wafers soaked in wine over my eyelids, a corner of my heart still aching for a miracle. I had done this many times, and each time there was no result. I had stopped believing that God could even work miracles. But that Sunday, my bones became feeble, as if the very thing that held them together had dissipated, and I asked God for a miracle.

For a huge part of my childhood, I felt like I was a piece of clockwork waiting to be fixed. The feelings started early, with the numerous appointments to eye specialists with my mother, trying to see if there was a way to cure my dancing eyes. "It is incurable" the doctor would say, and when we got home, my mother would wail, even though that doctor, like many other doctors, simply confirmed what she was told when I was born on that rainy Thursday in 1998.

Sometimes, a person might wish for a cure for reasons related to pain, discomfort, or life expectancy. Sometimes, a person might wish for a cure due to reasons related to how their disability intersects with their personal goals and lack of accessibility. Sometimes, a person might wish for a cure because of internalized ableism or a yearning to be accepted by others. A disabled person's feelings about a cure are never ours to assume or judge. The assumption that a disabled person wishes to be cured, and the words and actions born of that assumption, are what is ableist. Without nondisabled people perpetuating Disability as Something to Be Cured, people with disabilities are free to have autonomy in how they feel about their disability that isn't influenced by shame inflicted by others.

What Does This Look Like in Action? Manifestations of Disability as Something to Be Cured

1. Suggesting cures or treatments

When strangers ask about, or suggest, cures or treatments, the disabled person has to decide whether to respond with what they know, which can be an invasion of privacy, or to pretend they've never heard of it so they can say, "Oh, thanks, I'll look into that," and get out of the interaction faster. In most cases, many complexities are related to whether a potential "cure" would be appropriate, assuming that the person even wants a cure.

There have been times when Dan and I were out and a stranger asked if I have heard about some surgery that is restoring vision for some people. There is no intervention that would restore Dan's vision, so I haven't spent time researching surgeries. Even if I had, there is a deeper implication under the surface that I feel compelled to confront but usually don't have the energy for. In addition, I don't want to step into private medical information territory, which we will talk more about in chapter 11. However I answer that question, there will always be more to explain, and no matter how you slice it, it never feels like easy, breezy small talk that is appropriate to have with a stranger.

Challenge Yourself

First of all, remember that disabled people know far more about their disability than you do. Regardless of any good intentions in making a recommendation that you think could be helpful, in doing so, you are also implying that the person has not thoroughly explored their disability. If you really feel compelled to ask about or share a resource, ask the person first. "Are you up for a few questions about what you have already tried?" If the person declines, don't treat them as if they are being rude.

Second, don't assume that a disabled person would want a cure. If you are genuinely curious and wish to learn more, researching the cure you were thinking of suggesting is never off the table. But you can research it on your own time, rather than requiring the disabled person you are casually interacting with to educate you. To find disabled people who wish to use their energy to educate, you can do online research, and there are numerous resources in this book that you can look into further as well. By seeking education from those sources, you are not only supporting the work of disabled people but also accessing information they have chosen to share. Often, you will find a plethora of information about the disability that the author experiences, including information about whether there are treatments or cures, in their articles and memoirs.

How do you address talk of treatments or cures with your kids? Putting in the work to model acceptance of disability will be the first step. I have noticed that when kids have the knee-jerk reaction that Dan's blindness is sad, they will often ask a question related to the possibility of a cure. The child at the playground referenced in the previous chapter who said "That's pretty cool" didn't ask about a cure, though, because . . . it's cool. If your child does ask a question about a cure or fix, consider asking them what they think needs to be fixed and why. This will encourage deeper thought, allow you to address their specific understanding, and provide the opportunity to reiterate that many disabled people do not want to change or fix their disability because they don't consider it to be a problem. You can add that there are some people who hope for cures for certain conditions, but that information is usually private and personal, and it is best not to ask about cures unless you are close to the person.

2. Assuming that all disabled people are interested in cures

Assuming that disabled people will be pleased by measures that give the illusion of a cure without explicitly talking to them about it is a manifestation of Disability as Something to Be Cured. Assuming that your recently engaged friend who uses a wheelchair will be moved by the video you send them that shows a wheelchair user standing for her wedding is an example of what this can look like. I'm not suggesting that a wheelchair user standing for her wedding isn't a beautiful and important moment for some but, rather, suggesting that it isn't important for everyone and assuming such can be hurtful.

This manifestation was addressed by the Netflix show *Raising Dion*, which is about a child, Dion, with superpowers who has ADHD and chronic asthma. In the show, the main character's best friend, Esperanza, is a wheelchair user. Prior to Dion and Esperanza becoming best friends, Dion tried to distance himself from her in an attempt to impress the "cool kids." Later in the season, after Dion and Esperanza had connected on a deeper level, jealousy related to Esperanza's friendship with another child inspired Dion to use his superpowers to lift Esperanza out of her wheelchair without her consent. In an article written in December 2019 for *RaceBaitr*, "This 'Raising Dion' Story-Line Is a Powerful Lesson on Consent, Disability, and Possession," Amber Butts discusses this episode.

> Though they are in grave danger, Dion can't get his mind off of what he did to Esperanza the previous day.
>
> Nicole tries to comfort her son by telling him Esperanza will forgive him, but Dion's not convinced. He tries contacting Esperanza several times to apologize and she doesn't respond. Finally, when Nicole shares a story about how his godfather Pat didn't respect her wishes when she shared

that she didn't want to be in a relationship with him, things click for Dion.

"I think I didn't respect Esperanza's boundaries. I lifted her up out of her chair with magic. I thought she'd like it."

"Well, did she ever talk about wanting to get out of her chair?" Nicole responds.

Butts goes on to add:

> Dion's solution to re-animate his friendship with Esperanza came from a place of naïveté and ableism, not unfamiliar from his previous behavior of distancing himself from her. The reason he pushed for that distance had a lot to do with the shame he felt navigating his own disabilities (and how his peers might perceive them). In both cases, Dion made the false assumption that disability was a thing to be fixed.

We have talked to Dan about blindness and how his blindness will never be fixed. His feelings about whether he wishes there was a cure vary, but we have never wavered in our stance that we love him exactly as he is. If a cure somehow becomes available and he chooses to pursue it, we will give him our full support. That will be because it is what he wants, though, and not because we think that he would be better if he could see. The difference is key and at the heart of why conversations about cures that aren't pursued and driven by the person with a disability are problematic.

Challenge Yourself

If you are considering using your superpowers to momentarily cure a friend's disability, make sure to ask first. (Ha! I couldn't resist.) In all seriousness, before sending a disabled friend an article or video related to a fix or cure for a different person who shares their disability, reflect first on what you know about your friend's personal feelings about disability and on whether your friend has given any indication that they might be interested. Don't simply rely on the knowledge that your friend has a disability in common with the person in the story who cured or pushed back against their disability.

3. Asking, or demanding, to pray for a disabled person

I have read many accounts by disabled people sharing experiences of a stranger asking to pray for their healing. In some cases, when the disabled person declines, the stranger either starts praying anyway or argues with the disabled person, questioning why they don't want to be cured.

Someone once told me that he and his child had been praying for Dan's blindness to be healed. While I understood this came from a good but misinformed place, I knew this was my opportunity to provide some education. I explained that, with accommodations and access, Dan is not at a disadvantage. I explained that we don't pray for a cure but, rather, that people's understanding and acceptance of disability will improve so that the barriers that he faces will be reduced, which will lead to him being loved, accepted, and fully supported just as he is.

Challenge Yourself

A person's religion or faith has a lot to do with this manifestation. The power of prayer is a big deal to many people, and to pray for another is a gesture of care and concern. Given that some disabled people do not wish for a cure, though, going about this gesture in a different way might help the care and concern you are hoping to convey be best received. I am a Christian, and so, for a moment, I am going to share my personal opinions about answered prayers. This opinion and understanding of faith is mine and mine alone.

Dan is just as God made him, and we don't wish him any other way. To me, as a parent of a disabled child, answered prayers look like others improving their understanding and acceptance of him just as he is and taking steps to support him. Improved accessibility and nonableist attitudes about disability are literally answered prayers. Those who learn about marginalized people and put in work to care for them in ways that will be meaningful *are* answering prayers. I believe that prayers can be answered when people compelled by something bigger than themselves take action, even when it doesn't directly benefit them.

If someone notices that there isn't a safe way for my blind child to cross the street near our house and reaches out to the city, and the city puts in an accessible crossing feature, then a prayer of mine has been answered. An alternative to a church congregation praying for a church member's hearing to be restored would be a congregation who accepts d/Deafness and feels moved to collectively learn some sign language so that the member can feel welcome and communicate with others in the way that is most comfortable. A congregation who show care and concern by learning sign language will also be sending a message to other d/Deaf people in their community, showing by their actions, "We love you and want you here." In my opinion, there is always a place for prayer, but what you are praying for matters.

Bring It Home

In the book *We've Got This*, a collection of stories by disabled parents edited by Eliza Hull, Sam Drummond shares the complexity of the feelings he experienced when wondering whether his daughter would inherit his disability.

> If she does not have a disability, I have grieved for the part
> of her life that will miss out on the wonderful perspective
> and experiences that disability can bring. If she does have a
> disability, I have grieved for the part of her life that will be
> defined by society's prejudice and expectations.

When our tendency is to jump to thinking about how a disabled person might cease to be disabled, we miss out on the human in front of us and send the message that we don't fully accept them as they are. Disabled people experience life in a unique way and, as a result, bring unique experiences and perspectives. When we recognize these perspectives and experiences, and hold them in the same regard as those of nondisabled people, we will no longer see the need for a cure and can instead see facets of disability as aspects of individuality to be embraced.

In the children's book *Some Brains: A Book Celebrating Neurodiversity*, author Nelly Thomas highlights examples of how variations in neurology can bring beautiful perspectives and skills.

> I see letters fall from the page. Leah knows everything about
> the Ice Age.
>
> Jan sees numbers swirling in circles, and can even smell
> purple!
>
> If you want a great idea, have me on your team, I'll
> show you an angle, you probably won't see.
>
> (My neuro is not typical—that's why you need me!)

When you acknowledge that disabled people are valuable members of our communities, just as they are, your kids will not see disability as something that needs to be cured.

6

"MY DISABLED FRIEND, JOE"

TOKENIZING DISABILITY

I'm starting to see an upside to this. Let's say we take him out for the day with us, and we run into some ladies. They'll see us walking around with some poor dud, taking him under our wings, accepting him when no one else will, and we look like heroes.

THIS IS FROM ANOTHER SCENE from the video *Jeremy the Dud*, in which a double amputee and a man with dwarfism discuss the main character, a nondisabled and neurotypical "dud." While this is obviously very tongue-in-cheek, it isn't that far off from how disabled people are often treated, though people most often tokenize subconsciously. When someone references or uses a disabled person to make others think a certain way about them, that is an example of Tokenizing Disability. In this example, the two young men were counting on the ableism that makes people assign sainthood to those who spend time with disabled people to gain favor.

This doesn't just happen with individual people but is also perpetuated by groups. Consider for a moment that most disabled people report facing ableism in most settings and with many people they interact with. Next, consider how often you see organizations putting pictures of disabled people on their brochures or sharing stories with the media about how they so selflessly lifted up some disabled person. There is a great discrepancy between how often disabled people are shown as included in spaces and how often disabled people report feeling supported in those same spaces.

If an organization or company uses pictures of disabled people on its website with some sort of inspirational message about making space for everyone but employs very few disabled people and does not take employee reports of ableism in its place of business seriously, then that is an example of tokenizing. In these cases, the company or organization is using disabled people to generate favor. If an organization truly upholds inclusive practices and anti-ableist policies and is taking actionable steps to make improvements, then it is actively using its platform in a way that is nonableist and actually supportive.

I also want to make a note about representation, as it can sometimes get tangled up with tokenizing. Representation is complex, and context matters. It is important to consider the reason disability is being included in a situation. Disabled people seeing disability represented in the world they live in matters. Disability has historically been excluded from many systems and industries, including entertainment, advertising, employment, and education. The shift that is happening to increase disability representation is significant, but because of how ableism is often perpetuated and used by these systems and industries, it is important to understand the difference between representation and tokenization.

If a retailer includes disabled people in its advertising, is that tokenizing? I think it depends. Does the advertising include elements of inspiration, or are disabled people simply being included because they represent 15 to 30 percent of the population? Does the product or service advertised accommodate the disabilities shown? When a movie centers a disabled character, does the story avoid ableism in the arc of the character, and is the actor cast for the role disabled or nondisabled? These questions can help us understand the difference between proper representation and tokenizing.

Another way that disability is tokenized is when a person's disability becomes the only part of them acknowledged or recognized. In *Have Dog, Will Travel*, Stephen Kuusisto writes about how his blindness became the center of discussion when attending an arts retreat.

> I was in the dining room at a prestigious arts retreat, in a room where Yoko Ono once ate spaghetti and instead of discussing the arts, I was describing light—that the blind can often see it, that many see colors. And that those who don't see anything at all still understand the world richly.

In a November 2022 post on my education and advocacy Facebook page, which is called iNFORM, I wrote the following:

> What I wish for is a world where strangers are more likely to simply say "hi" to my son or extend a compliment about his shirt or shoes than they are to ask about his disability. . . . Because it's bad to talk about disability? No. Because a 9yo would much rather talk about his favorite things.

It is rare for strangers we encounter in public to talk to Dan (or me, when we are together) about something other than his disability.

If we have a casual interaction with a stranger and Dan's blindness doesn't come up at all, I consider it a miracle.

What Does This Look Like in Action? Manifestations of Tokenizing Disability

1. Mentioning a person's disability when irrelevant to the matter at hand

A person's disability doesn't always need to be discussed. When it is brought into a conversation unnecessarily, Tokenizing Disability might be at work. If someone said, "My friend Joe is coming to the party tonight, and he survived a traumatic brain injury. He is sensitive to sudden, loud noises, so avoid yelling, if you can," that would be an example of providing an accommodation. In such cases, it is important that Joe has disclosed this fact about himself and has given permission to the party host to disclose it to others for the sake of accommodation. Alternately, if someone said, "My friend Joe is coming to the party tonight, and he survived a traumatic brain injury. He's my hero," that person would most likely be guilty of tokenizing Joe. In this example, the reason for bringing up Joe's traumatic brain injury does not seem to be serving any purpose other than stirring emotion in the other person. The intention might be to evoke feelings of pity for, or inspiration about, Joe. Another potential intention could be to evoke feelings of admiration or acclaim for the party host for being friends with and inviting a disabled person to the party. In this case, disclosing Joe's medical history might not be what he would want and seems to be being used to stir emotion about Joe that he might not be comfortable with.

Challenge Yourself

If you have disabled people in your life, only include their disability in conversation with others if it is pertinent or relevant. If you plan to talk about your disabled friend to others, give careful thought to your reasons and be sure to have conversations with your friend first. In many cases, there isn't any reason to share information about a person's disability. It isn't necessarily that the person doesn't want people to know about it, but when you make a point to identify someone's disability, it makes the disability the conversation topic. Some disabled people might enjoy talking about their disability, and if that's the case, then they should be the ones to start the conversation, especially among strangers.

2. Disability being the only recognized aspect of a person

A disabled person's disability being suggested to be their entire identity is another manifestation of Tokenizing Disability. During episode 101 of the podcast *The Accessible Stall*, hosts Emily Ladau and Kyle Khachadurian discuss how, though they are disabled 24/7, they do not wish to be reminded of their disability constantly. Kyle explains, "It is something that is entirely part of me, but it is also one part of me. And it's the one part of me that affects everything else that I do." He goes on to say, "I feel like the world pigeonholes me and I don't want to be pigeonholed."

Challenge Yourself

If you encounter disabled people in public and wish to engage with them, it is entirely acceptable to just do what you normally do when you casually interact with people. If you are a person who likes to make small talk about something specific, realize that commenting on a person's clothing or the weather is still on the table if the person has a disability. Consider that because it is so common for a disabled person's disability to be the topic of conversation, not bringing it up will be perfectly acceptable.

If disabled people address their disability, certainly follow their lead. Allowing them to be humans simply doing life sounds like something very simple but is rarer than you think.

3. Underrepresentation and misrepresentation of disability in entertainment

In entertainment, it is rare to see disabled actors. When you do see them, it is rare to see their disability not being the focal point of their character. Usually, disabled people are included in entertainment solely for purposes related to disability and rarely simply because they represent 15 to 30 percent of the population. The same is true in children's books. Although the situation is improving, it is still rare to find children's books that are not specifically about disability or social justice that include pictures of disabled children or disabled characters. The trend related to disability representation in media and entertainment is another manifestation of Tokenizing Disability.

Don't get me wrong. I think stories about disability are important. But when disabled people exist only in stories about disability, it's a problem. Even though disabled people spend all their time living life while disabled, their disability is not their primary focus every minute of every day, as was expressed earlier by Kyle Khachadurian.

See Jane is an organization that researches representation in media and supports initiatives to improve the disparities that exist. A 2020 report called "See Jane 2020 Film: Historic Gender Parity in Family Films" indicated that 8 percent of feature films in 2019 featured a lead with a disability, which was up from 1 percent, where it had previously been for decades. The report also indicated that disabled characters were more likely to be rescued (34.3 percent as compared to 20.6 percent for nondisabled characters) or die (20 percent as compared to 11.7 percent for nondisabled characters).

Challenge Yourself

If you are a person who creates work that will be viewed by a larger public, keep disability representation in mind. As a consumer of media, show your support for improvements in disability representation by exploring media that includes disabled actors. At the very least, don't discount it *because* it includes disabled actors.

When it comes to your kids, seeing disability more regularly will be important for their ability to reject ableism and not internalize disability as something to single out. Make an effort to boost their access to disability representation in their toys, books, media, and activities. In addition, look for opportunities to support anti-ableism in your kids' play. In a December 2022 post on the website PDA Our Way, a page run by neurodivergent blogger Dannii Bolton, is a picture of a baby doll with no arms wearing a pink baby hat with a bow, rainbow onesie, and bib with small triangles on it. The post says:

> We are having a massive, very necessary end of year house clean up. While elbow deep in the overflowing toy basket I declared, "I will be throwing out all toys with broken parts and missing limbs." My nine year old turned to me immediately and called me out, "That is ableist, Mum, and frankly not very compassionate either." Neurokindred, the shift is happening and I'm so here for it!

This post reminded me of when Pete was three or four and we found one of his Power Ranger action figures with a leg missing. We used a part we found in the toy box to make him a prosthetic leg and he got right back to fighting. Including disability as a normal part of their play is another good way to empower your kids to recognize ableism and reject it. Retailers are making more and more toys that represent disability, and there aren't any rules that state only disabled kids can own them. Diversifying your kids' toy box is an actionable step you can take.

4. Tokenizing in the name of justice

Have you ever been scrolling social media and come across an article about someone with a disability that didn't sit well with you? Maybe the story was about discrimination or exclusion, abuse, or misunderstanding. You connect with the story because you have a relationship with someone who has the same disability as the person in the article. You want others to know about the story and how what happened was wrong, so you decide to share it. Nothing wrong with that! Instead of sharing it as is, though, you decide to tag and/or mention your disabled friend, along with statements of how you would be utterly appalled if they were treated that way.

In the spirit of supporting your friend with a disability, you have tokenized them. Was it your intention to tokenize them? Certainly not. My best guess is that our impulse to do this may be connected to credibility. It's like saying, "I am qualified to take this stance because of this friend of mine." The question I would like you to consider is: Do you have to have a personal connection to take a stance on something? Do you have to have a personal connection to bullying to be against bullying?

Tokenizing seems to be most common when it comes to marginalized groups. It's almost as if people think they need permission to take a stance that they think society might deem controversial. Maybe they think they are less likely to get pushback when sharing a personal connection. Your motivation might be connected to a specific person you care about, but that person may or may not be comfortable with this gesture.

Challenge Yourself

Stand up for what you think is right, but don't tokenize any person or group while doing so. If you are debating whether to attach friends or family members to your advocacy effort, make sure to ask them first and keep in mind the position it puts them in. Be sure to make it clear that you won't be upset if they aren't comfortable with being included.

5. Using a personal relationship with a disabled person to excuse individual ableism

This manifestation is not exclusive to ableism—and, in fact, you have probably heard it associated with the treatment of other marginalized groups. The formula has wide application, though. How often have you heard, "I'm not racist/sexist/homophobic/xenophobic/ableist. My family member/friend is [marginalized group]."

The implication is that having a personal relationship with some-one from a marginalized group makes a person incapable of perpetuat-ing a microaggression toward that group. I suppose the foundations behind this manifestation include a few factors:

1. a person who has not opened themselves up to the idea of the harmful biases that exists in them, and thus have done nothing to combat them AND
2. that person not taking the time to consider that their friend from a marginalized group has a very different lived experience than they do AND
3. that person genuinely does not wish to cause any hurt or harm to their friend.

In an article called "Hey, Your 'Black Friend' Here—Stop Using Me," author Leenika Belfield-Martin writes, "Your personal relationships with Black people don't magically opt you out from having racist tendencies, nor do they end the systematic racism your Black friends face. It takes more. Yes, you may be friends, but what do you do to be actively antiracist?"

All of this is true for ableism. When people do not take the time to identify and confront the ableism inside of them, they will perpetuate ableism in their friendships and relationships with disabled people. Though the specifics of the ways that marginalized groups are treated differs, bias, stigma, and sometimes fear are the driving forces for all. For that reason, the work required to be better, for all marginalized groups, includes paradigm shifts and deconstruction of old ideas and misconceptions.

Challenge Yourself

Remember that your relationship with a disabled person, or disabled people, does not negate ableism. That relationship means that you have a personal connection to disability, but if you are nondisabled, you still lack lived experience as a disabled person. If your disabled friend or family member has never talked to you about ableism before, that does not mean that they do not experience ableism. It might mean that they have not yet felt you are safe enough to be open with, or it might be that it just has not come up.

If you have perpetuated ableism in their presence, like making a disability joke, it is possible that they have laughed or said nothing. If they laughed along, that doesn't mean the joke was not ableist, and it does not mean that it did not offend them. It might have offended them and it might not have, but their reaction is not always indicative of how they felt about it. Disabled people are often put in the position of feeling pressured to accept ableism, as pushing back on it could mean confrontation or loss of relationship. Many disabled people know that their friends and family members do not mean personal harm, and therefore it is easier to say nothing than to speak up.

If a disability-related issue arises and you desire to hear how your disabled friend/family member feels about it, you can always ask if they feel comfortable talking about it. Keep in mind, though, that one disabled person's opinion is one person's opinion. Avoid assuming that the way your personal connection to a marginalized group feels is representative of all members of that group.

When it comes to your kids, putting in the work to set the example of treating people with disabilities as individuals, and setting the standards of speaking respectfully about disability, will reduce the likelihood of perpetuating ableism in the first place. Older children are likely to understand the foundations of this manifestation if you talk it through with them. It is possible that they have talked about this form of tokenizing connected to another marginalized group, so it will be easy to help them see the similarities.

Bring It Home

If a child can understand why pity and inspiration are inappropriate to apply to disabled people, you can explain that tokenizing is when someone understands that people feel that way and then uses those feelings for their own gain.

Take notice of what your kids pay attention to and see if disability is represented. Are there disabled characters in the books they read or shows they watch? By taking many of the steps we have already talked about, like not talking about your kids' disabled peers differently and not going out of your way to point out disability unless it is to educate about ableism, you will naturally steer your kids away from tokenizing. When you see examples of tokenizing, take the time to talk to your kids about it.

Tokenizing happens when someone views another human as a unit, or token, rather than as a human. If you posture disability as a normal part of the human condition and refrain from tokenizing, your kids are more likely to see tokenizing as inappropriate. There is a beautiful children's book called *All Are Welcome* by Alexandra Penfold and Suzanne Kaufman. The book is not about disability but rather about community—a very diverse community that includes disability, among other marginalized groups. There are disabled characters in the book in places like art class, at the lunch table, and on the playground, which is exactly where disabled people exist—*everywhere*.

Open doors, rush outside. We will swing. We will slide. We'll have fun side by side.

All are welcome here.

We're part of a community. Our strength is our diversity. A shelter from adversity.

All are welcome here.

7

"DISABLED PEOPLE HAVE KIDS?"

STEREOTYPING DISABILITY

———

IN A VIDEO ON THE WEBSITE Facing History & Ourselves called "How Stereotypes Affect Us and What We Can Do," Claude Steele, a provost at the University of California, Berkely, talks about stereotype threat.

> So some forms of this threat are pretty minor and almost humorful, and other forms of this threat are really poignant. One thing to say in a Facing History context is that stereotypes are one way by which history affects present life, because stereotypes are built up over the history of a society. And they can have an impact on people's functioning in the immediate, present situations, and are big factors in the way our society functions. Who goes into what fields, who enjoys what kind of work. These things are driven, in big part, by these kinds of threats.

Disabled people report a wide variety of stereotypes that perpetuate and fuel ableism. In addition to the stereotypes that are highlighted throughout this book, countless additional stereotypes pervade and persist. An article by Laurie Block of the Disability History Museum, "Stereotypes About People with Disabilities," lists the following stereotypes:

- Disabled people are limited, partial, or lesser.
- The successful disabled person is "superhuman."
- Disabled people are a menace to themselves, to others, and to society.
- The families of the disabled are "noble sacrificers."

Additional stereotypes I have come across in my research include the following (a nonexhaustive list):

- Disabled people don't get married.
- Disabled people can't live independently.
- Disability only affects older people.
- All autistic people are savants.
- Everyone who has tics has Tourette's syndrome.
- People with Down syndrome are always happy.
- Immunocompromised people can just stay home to stay healthy.
- All d/Deaf people sign.
- Blind people like to touch faces.
- People who receive disability benefits are lazy.

In her book *Daddy Won't Let Mom Drive the Car*, Jo Elizabeth Pinto tells a story about a trip to the convenience store to buy a reward slurpie for her daughter who had aced a spelling test. They encountered a stranger in line.

> "I bet you help your mommy out a lot, don't you?"
> I winced inwardly. The man could have focused on the spelling test or the Slurpee®, but instead he had fixated on

my blindness and assumed my daughter took care of me. It happens a lot, and it doesn't get any less annoying with each occurrence.

"I guess I kinda help her," Sarah said. "When I feel like it."

That's true enough. Sarah, like any nine-year-old, can be quite helpful, when it suits her. She likes to operate the steam mop on our hardwood floors. Sometimes she enjoys giving me a hand with dinner preparations or baking brownies with me. She'll pitch in with yard work because she knows her dad and I usually take her out for ice cream when it's over. But she can make a mess as well as the next kid and be just as reluctant to clean it up, too. She's no saint because her mom is blind, nor would I want her to be.

"You know what?" the stranger in line decided. "Tell your mom to put her money away. I'm buying you that Slurpee®. I watched you two crossing the street, and you were very careful, not letting your mom walk out in front of cars or trip on the curb or anything."

Actually, I had listened for oncoming traffic and had determined when it was safe to cross the street, and my guide dog had paused at the curb so I wouldn't trip. I could have made the crossing safely on my own.

In this story, a stereotype related to disabled parents led to an ableist encounter that left the author annoyed, underestimated, and misrepresented. Is it possible that, in some cases, children of disabled parents provide some assistance to their parents? Definitely. I would expect so, since children of nondisabled parents sometimes provide help to their parents. The stereotype this stranger was operating on made him feel comfortable enough to determine it to be true for the author and her daughter, even though he knew nothing of their individual circumstances.

In a conversation on their Facebook page Squirmy and Grubs, inter-abled couple* Shane and Hannah Burcaw talk about some of the many misconceptions and stereotypes that have surfaced from their online presence. Shane explains:

> People see my attraction, my ability to attract a partner, as nonexistent. . . . When Hannah and I began our channel, we never really considered the idea that people would question our intimacy, our love, our romance. And, boy they did!

They go on to talk about many additional stereotypes regarding romantic relationships and intimacy in disability. These stereotypes essentially negate the possibility of love and intimacy for disabled people and also posit that nondisabled people in relationships with disabled people have questionable ethics.

In this chapter, I will not be addressing every single stereotype that exists. There is no need. Rather, my goal is to highlight some of the different ways that stereotypes can perpetuate harm.

Stereotyping Disability plays a large part in the employment challenges that disabled people face. In an article for Inclusively called "Disability Stereotypes That Won't Go Away," Matthew Shapiro writes:

> There's also this stigma that people with disabilities can only do food, flowers, or be custodians, essentially that they can only do food, flora, and filth, and that's also not an accurate assessment. Why can't people work in Fortune 500 companies if given the right accommodations and given the right

---

* *Inter-abled* refers to a romantic relationship that includes a disabled and a nondisabled person.

support? Why can't people with disabilities eventually, if they're put on the right track to be successful, be the CEO or CFO of a big business? And why can't they start their own businesses?

In the *Washington Post* article "Why No One Will Hire Me," Chuck Jones describes what it has been like to search for a job as a man with a physical disability.

> Although discrimination in hiring the disabled is illegal, as codified in the Americans With Disabilities Act, it nevertheless occurs. I am a case in point. I'm a one-legged man, and I can't get a job.
>
> In February 2005 I lost my leg to cancer, a sarcoma on my right tibia. I walk with the aid of a prosthesis and a cane. I can walk, stand for prolonged periods, go up and down stairs, and drive a car. By trade, I'm a writer and editor—office work. I have more than 23 years of professional experience. I have an impressive portfolio and have won awards.
>
> Yet employers will not touch me.

He explains the typical progression in his job searches and how the interest and enthusiasm about him as a candidate gradually increase until the in-person interview, after which point he is notified that another candidate has been selected. He goes on:

> I realize that active prejudice is probably not in play in these situations. Human nature is. Think of it: If you're a company looking at your bottom line and you're faced with two candidates of equal skills—one has a disability and one does not, whom would you choose?

This is just my story. But most people with disabilities who are able and willing to work have similar tales. It's not fair, but that's the way it is.

What Does This Look Like in Action? Manifestations of Stereotyping Disability

1. Assuming that all disabled people have the same opinions and preferences

Taking one disabled person's views, needs, or experiences and applying them to more than just that person is a manifestation of Stereotyping Disability that is sometimes described as "lumping." In *Sitting Pretty*, Rebekah Taussig writes:

> I am not—by any stretch of the imagination—the representative of all disabled people. That's not a thing. The fact that I have a very visible disability (turns out it's difficult to overlook a wheelchair), and the fact that I was disabled at a very young age, changes the way you and I experience this body of mine. Even folks who share these same traits will have their own slant on what it means to them, because the experience of disability is as varied as the experiences of childbirth or breakups—there are at least seven billion different ways this could go, and even within one person, feelings can contradict or change over time. Disability expands into every possible corner and intersects with every possible identity. I would be doing all of us a great disservice if I led you to believe that the conversation starts and ends with bodies and experiences that look just like mine.

It is very important to understand that each disabled person is an individual with unique experiences, perspectives, and circumstances.

Challenge Yourself

Listening to a variety of disabled voices is important because, as Rebekah explains, experiences of disabled people vary on an individual basis. If you have experience with one disabled person or have more knowledge about one disability, avoid using that experience or knowledge to make generalizations about other disabled people and disabilities. Don't rely on a stereotype to fill in any blanks for you. Instead, acquire necessary information on an individual basis.

In regard to interactions I have had on behalf of Dan, I have appreciated when people have reached out if they are unsure about what Dan might need or prefer, rather than making assumptions based on stereotypes about blind people. There have been times when someone was considering a very well-intentioned gesture that would not have been beneficial for Dan, and that person might have felt discouraged, or even resentful, if the gesture was not considered to be a success.

2. Stereotypes that shape perceptions about disabled people in relationships

Many stereotypes exist regarding the partners of disabled people. It is sometimes assumed that a disabled person's partner will be responsible for their care, are burdened by them, and/or are with the disabled person out of pity. Sometimes, partners of disabled people do provide care, and we must understand that the feelings of caregiver partners are personal. On her page Wheelchair Rapunzel, Alex Dacy shared about when she and her boyfriend attended the Spinal Muscular Atrophy Conference together. She posted that her boyfriend surprised her by telling her that he was going to attend the caregiver's toolbox and that he was very excited to go from poster to poster, talking to scientists about her disease. She said, "Later that night we had a beau-tiful deep conversation, and the way he was so incredibly involved and interested in my disease made me love him that much more."

In November 2022, social media blogger Uncle Tics, who shares his experiences with Tourette's syndrome, posted a Facebook Reel that includes him and his girlfriend, Olivia, responding to a question asked by a follower: "Do you and Livvy want to have kids?" They both answer yes, and then Uncle Tics adds, "I will be honest, though. Only a few years ago, I didn't want kids." He asks Olivia, "Do you know why?" She answers, "You felt that you didn't want your kids to have your disability and to suffer." He responds, "I didn't want kids for f——ing years, and it was Olivia that changed my mind on it." Later he goes on to say, "Anyway, to wrap this up. We would love to have kids. I'm just scared my kids are gonna suffer like I did." Olivia responds, "They won't. They've got good parents."

The ableism that perpetuates the stereotype that disabled people cannot have loving partnerships is the same ableism that can lead a disabled person to feel as if they will never find such a partnership or, worse, that they are undeserving of one. Disabled people are lovable and deserving of love, and a disabled person finding love isn't any more miraculous than a nondisabled person finding love. In addition, the partner of a disabled person loving and caring for them in ways specific to their needs is no different than how partners of a nondis-abled people care for the individual needs of their partner. Attaching an implication of obligation or hardship when one of the people in the relationship is disabled is ableism.

Challenge Yourself

If you were operating under the stereotype that disabled people are bur-dens to their caregivers, you can shift your mindset, because now you know better. Don't act surprised when you hear stories of disabled people in committed partnerships, and don't be more, or less, excited about them than you would about any other story of love and partnership.

3. Disability tropes in entertainment that misinform

TVtropes.org collects an extensive list of tropes commonly portrayed in fiction. Some examples are "Attention Deficit . . . Ooh, Shiny!," "Blind People Wear Sunglasses," "Disability Alibi," and "Wheelchair Antics." These tropes can be very harmful for people with disabilities. Entertainment is powerful, and perpetuated stereotypes fuel their continuation.

In the episode of *Open Stutter* on YouTube that was referenced in chapter 3, Aliza shares how stereotypes about stuttering make her feel.

> It's just really frustrating, because the way that the world shows people who stutter in movies or comic strips or anything, it's just so stigmatized as you're unintelligent or you don't know what you're talking about or you're less capable than other people, so . . . it's just frustrating trying to prove everyone wrong.

Challenge Yourself

When you see disability stereotypes in media, point them out to your kids. Help them break down what might be relevant to the storyline and appropriate versus what might have been added for entertainment value at the expense of the disabled person or people who have the disability represented through stereotypes.

4. Disability stereotypes that affect employment

A February 2022 report by the Bureau of Labor Statistics of the US Department of Labor reported that the unemployment rates for disabled people actively seeking employment were two times higher than the rates for nondisabled people.

In *Just Human*, Arielle Silverman speaks to additional factors that influence employment for disabled people.

> Negative attitudes among employers certainly abound. In a 2014 survey of 181 hiring managers, for example, two-thirds of the respondents could not explain how a blind employee accesses print, uses industrial equipment, uses a computer, or uses a cash register. Employers may mistakenly believe, not only that blind employees could not do their jobs well, but that blind employees would be too expensive to accommodate or too much of an insurance liability. In a post-ADA world, such attitudes may lead to covert discrimination or, in some cases, more overt discrimination.

When employers or hiring managers are undereducated about disability, they might fill in the blanks using stereotypes. "Blind candidates are not qualified because they can't read the e-mails and reports that are part of the job description" is an example of the conclusion someone might come to when undereducation and stereotypes work in tandem. What that person might really mean is "I don't know that a blind person can access assistive technology and accessibility features to read e-mails and reports and am using this misunderstanding to confirm why blind people can't find jobs."

When it comes to employment, stereotypes can essentially make a disabled person disappear. What the disabled person can actually do is never considered, because she has been ruled out based on conclusions that she isn't given the chance to prove or disprove.

Challenge Yourself

If you are a person in charge of hiring or have influence over employment at your place of work, be explicit in confronting your own biases. If you have concerns about a disabled candidate's ability to handle a specific responsibility of the job based on assumptions you are making, address those concerns directly with the candidate by asking. Assuming takes away the candidate's right to show competence. Be open to the importance of accommodations and try not to let the possibility of necessary accommodations deter you from considering a disabled candidate. Not only is discrimination against the law, but it could also be blocking you from considering someone who might be great in the position. Oftentimes, accommodations can be established fairly quickly and easily and soon become commonplace.

Am I suggesting that you always hire the disabled person? Not at all. That would just be ableism of a different shade. Passing on the disabled candidate rather than taking the time to ask a few additional questions and opening your mind to possibility is actively working against practices and structures that disabled people need society to adopt to ensure more fairness and inclusivity. More employers willing to seriously consider disabled candidates will lead to more disabled people employed, which will lead to higher visibility of disabled employees, which will lead to younger generations seeing disability more in their communities. Seeing disabled people serving a variety of roles in their communities will dispel the stereotype that disabled people don't work, as the stereotypes that lead to employment challenges fuel other stereotypes.

Bring It Home

Stereotypes are developed through assumptions that are asserted in a number of different ways. Some stereotyping happens subconsciously, as a result of what we absorb from our environment. In terms of what stereotypes you should pass along to your kids, I can't answer that question. The more that I have learned personally, the more I try to avoid all stereotypes, good and bad. What I do think might be helpful, though, is encouraging your kids to apply a degree of questioning and critical thinking when encountering stereotypes. Applying assumptions broadly manifests as ableism in many ways, and stereotyping is no exception.

If encountering a stereotype, you can encourage your child to break it down: "Do you think it is possible for every person in a defined group to be the same in any specific way? Are there some ways that could be a yes but others that are probably a no? Why?"

Another way to help our kids learn to challenge stereotypes is through the experiences and resources that we provide them.

> This is a story about living joyfully as you are, without any
> limitations or expectations of how others may see you. Gato
> is many things and can never be confined to a narrow box.

That text appears on the inside sleeve of the book *Not a Cat: A Memoir* by Winter Miller. In this delightful children's book, the main character expresses that the label of *cat* doesn't feel sufficient and encourages the reader to apply skepticism.

> I run in pastures, so how do you know I'm not a horse?
> Sometimes I eat grass. Maybe I'm a cow? . . . I love flowers,
> just like a bee. Hey! I swim in a lake! What if I'm a duck?

This book provokes thought not only regarding complexity and individuality but also about how different aspects of our individuality can be common ground with others. Introducing and encouraging this type of thinking will lay a foundation that naturally leads to questioning stereotypes.

8

"HEY, BUDDY"

INFANTILIZING DISABILITY

———————

MANY DISABLED PEOPLE report unbelievably frustrating encounters with strangers. A video on Open Future Learning's Facebook page from April 2022 aptly titled "Eye Roll" reenacts such an encounter. A disabled man approaches a ticket desk and asks for two tickets to a specific movie. The employee looks at the nondisabled person with him and tells her the total. She notes that the man will be paying. The employee then faces the man and repeats, "Seven pounds," louder and slower, while holding up seven fingers. He pays her and she tries to give his change to the woman, who points back to the man. The man says, "That's my money. My change." The employee apologizes and proceeds to slowly count back his change, one coin at a time, as she places each into his hand. She then puts both hands around his closed hand and says, "Keep that safe, OK?" before trying to hand the tickets to the woman, who again gestures toward the man. The employee then slowly says, "Here's your tickets," while handing the man his tickets before adding, "Well done. Enjoy the film." The woman treated this grown man like you might treat a five-year-old child who is using his own money at the gas station for the first time to buy candy. This is an example of the infantilization that many people with disabilities report experiencing.

Infantilizing Disability happens when disabled people are treated as being much younger than they actually are. This form of ableism tells us the lie that disabled people are akin to children, regardless of their age or individual needs, and should be treated as such. In February 2022, Sofia Jirau, a twenty-four-year-old Puerto Rican model, announced that she would be the first Victoria's Secret model with Down syndrome. Many people were excited about this barrier being broken down, but naturally, ableism showed up in full force. In an article written for the *Unwritten* following the announcement, "Disabled Women Like Victoria's Secret Model Sofia Jirau Don't Need You to Protect Them," Melissa Parker, a disabled freelance journalist, addressed the ableism regarding Sofia's breakthrough.

> Across social media, and in comments sections, the move has been labeled "exploitive."
>
> Jirau worked for this position, so, to have nondisabled people suggest that she didn't—or that she could not consent to it, to have strangers question the severity of her disability, and to have them indicate that it was a perversion to involve her, is disgusting.
>
> "Not sure how I feel about this," "So wrong," "But they're like a child." "She needs someone to watch her in that room." read the comments.
>
> The infantilization is vile. She's not a child. She is a disabled woman. Outsiders do not have to be "sure" about our choices. We're not looking for validation from nondisabled people—our lives would be somewhat stunted if that were

the case. We would exist in a perpetual state of childhood, never quite reaching puberty or shedding our purity.

Disabled adults have a right to autonomy and self-determination, and suggesting that they should not be allowed to make adult choices is ableist. Infantilization is also at work when it is implied that disabled people cannot be held responsible or accountable for their actions. In season 6, episode 1 of the show *Orange Is the New Black*, there is a scene in which two inmates are found hiding in a closet. When discovered by two guards, they pretend to be deaf to try to avoid harsh treatment. After the two inmates start pretending to sign, one of the guards says, "They got deaf people in here? Wonder what they did." The other guard responds, "Ableist! Deaf people can crime like anybody else."*

In an article written in December 2015 for Everyday Feminism, "Don't Call my Sister 'Cute': 6 Good Reasons to Stop Infantilizing Disabled People," Creigh Farinas shares the experience of observing her disabled sister being infantilized. Creigh writes:

> As soon as she'd gathered enough data to dump Caley into her brain's "disabled" category, my acquaintance had immediately switched to baby speech. She'd spoken very slowly, exaggerating every word, took her vocabulary down a few notches, and responded with overacted enthusiasm to every phrase that came out of Caley's mouth. At one point, she literally patted Caley on the head. And, what's more, every few sentences or so, my acquaintance would look up at me with a bright smile and utter that damning phrase: "Your sister's so cute!"

---

* Pretending to be disabled is generally insensitive, and I'm not sure how d/Deaf people feel about this aspect of the scene.

Dan has experienced Infantilizing Disability many times, but one memorable example happened when my two boys were playing at a park in another state on a trip to visit family. They had been exploring the playground equipment, but I noticed they were walking toward me, hand in hand. I heard Pete tell Dan, "Come on, let's go check this out over here, by Mom." Pete shot me a look and I knew something was wrong. He guided Dan to a ladder that was attached to the playground structure closest to me and then stomped toward me. I asked him what was wrong. He came close to me and in an angry whisper said, "That girl over there is treating Dan like he's a baby. He's not a baby. She is being so rude! I need to go take a walk." I told him to take the time he needed and that I would stick close to Dan and monitor what was going on.

I noticed that the little girl Pete had pointed out had come to the equipment that Dan was now on, so I moved closer so I could hear what was being said. The little girl was standing in front of Dan, who was casually exploring the equipment, and was saying, "Yoo-hoo. Over here. Yoo-hoo." It seemed that she was attempting to guide him through the equipment, even though he wasn't showing interest in her presence, let alone her help. I said, "You can just talk to him using words instead of making sounds. He can understand what you're saying." She followed that up with "You can do it! You've got this!" It was clear that she wanted to be helpful, and her interpretation of Dan's disability led her to believe that he needed to be treated like a very small child.

She was a kid and it made me giggle, partially because Dan wasn't paying any attention to her whatsoever, and shortly thereafter she went somewhere else to play. But prior to me telling her that he can understand words, she was communicating with him in a way similar to how you would interact with a lost dog. Later, Pete told me that she was using a patronizing, babyish tone with him while rolling her eyes and gesturing about him to a friend, since she knew that Dan couldn't see her. It is actually very common for other children to interact with Dan as if he is much younger than he is. Do I begrudge the children? Not at all. They only know what they have absorbed and been taught and don't know what they don't know. Instead, I focus on the education needed to empower children and their parents to learn how to do better.

When do people infantilize? The decision to infantilize is most likely a subconscious one and is based on a person's biases, prior experiences, and ablest notions that they have absorbed. A disabled person's physical appearance and behavior seem to be the primary factors that can lead to a person being infantilized. On the *Autism & ADHD Diaries* podcast from February 2021, host Danielle Punter talks to autistic writer Callum Stephen. Callum talks about how differently he and his sister are often treated, even though they are both disabled, due to differences in the way their disabilities can be detected and perceived by others. Danielle asks what assumptions are made about Callum and his sister. Callum answers:

> I think there's quite a lot of assumptions made about both of us. When it comes to myself and my autism, people often assume that I have, and this only means about why this is wrong, but I have mild autism and my sister would have "spicy autism" or something. And with that comes the assumption that I'm always OK, I don't experience any anxiety or any difficulties in life, that masking has no effect on me, that I'm naturally sociable, that I can do all of these things just as neurotypical people do it. Life doesn't affect me and that being different doesn't have an impact on my life. Whereas when it comes to my sister, the minute someone identifies her as supposedly "low functioning," they almost write her off and they think, "Oh, she can't do anything. She can't do this, she can't communicate," and it's this weird

disparity where everyone assumes that my life is perfect and really easy and I'm capable of anything and that I can't possibly need any support. Whereas when it comes to my sister, they all assume she needs support with absolutely everything and that she's incapable.

What Does This Look Like in Action? Manifestations of Infantilizing Disability

1. Acting differently during interactions with disabled people

Examples of infantilizing behavior applied to disabled people who are not small children can include the following:

- Changing voice volume and rate of speech to be louder and slower
- Using baby talk
- Using a singsong quality of speaking
- Using nicknames like "buddy," "bud," or "pal"
- Oversimplifying a message
- Using descriptors like "cute," "adorable," or "precious"
- Calling the person "sweetheart" or "sweetie"
- Patting the person on the head

Challenge Yourself

When interacting with a disabled adolescent or adult, don't alter your speech patterns, vocabulary, gestures, or physical proximity from those you would typically use with nondisabled adults. If it would be out of line for you to do with a nondisabled acquaintance of that age, then it is out of line to do with a disabled adolescent or adult. If you model typical interactions with disabled people for your children, this behavior will be their standard. If you witness examples of disabled people being infantilized, speak up if you are in an appropriate position to do so, and in a way that does not embarrass them or put them in a difficult position.

2. Treating someone as younger because of their interests

Blogger and writer Jess Wilson wrote a post about infantilizing on her Facebook page Diary of a Mom in December 2013.

> I am constantly aware of my propensity to infantilize my autistic daughter. The things that she relates to and enjoys are typically meant for much younger children. Her language is not, by any stretch, that of a typical fifth grader. She revels in toddler-style potty humor. She reads at a first-grade level. At a whopping 4′3″ and 57 pounds, she wears a size 7. She can slip into a group of second graders without a second glance.
>
> And yet, she is ten years old, soon to be eleven. She deserves as much freedom and independence as I can safely give her. She deserves the assumption of competence, of intellect, of an ability to understand . . . well, everything. She deserves exposure to every last thing the world has to offer, opportunities to push and stretch and explore, and respect for her preferences once she has. . . . My daughter deserves to be treated not as a toddler, but as herself.

Challenge Yourself

There is no need to make assumptions about a person based on what they like. Embrace the idea that there are no rules regarding what a person can be into. Any notions we have societally are constructs, and we don't have to buy into them. Don't treat someone differently because they are interacting with objects, or wearing clothing, that is marketed to younger people. Leaving more room for people to express individuality will benefit not just disabled people but everyone.

Don't be afraid to comment on or compliment someone, disabled or nondisabled, who is interacting with or wearing an interest of theirs, but make sure you aren't doing it in a way that is babyish or patronizing. If you wouldn't baby-talk nondisabled Bob about his Kansas City Chiefs T-shirt, don't baby-talk a disabled adult about a cartoon character on his T-shirt.

3. Functioning labels oversimplifying the humanity of people with disabilities

Have you ever heard the terms *high functioning* or *low functioning* in reference to disabled people? These are functioning labels, and they are now largely considered to be problematic by the disabled community. Sometimes people also use severity markers like *mild*, *moderate*, and *severe* in this way.

In an August 2020 article for Planning Across the Spectrum called "Here's Why You Should Stop Using Functioning Labels," three reasons are given for discontinuing the use of such labels: they are based on outdated science, they don't tell the whole story, and they are ableist. The article goes on:

> Functioning labels isolate disabled people from their nondisabled peers by implying defectiveness. They undercut one's individuality, struggles, and abilities—their *humanity*—and emphasize brokenness, reducing them to terms we'd use for a malfunctioning machine.

Challenge Yourself

Professionals who support disabled individuals have ways of sharing information for the purpose of providing appropriate support. Having appropriate terminology is necessary for collaboration and care coordination in certain settings and contexts. Those ways of sharing information have moved, or are moving, away from functioning labels.

Outside of situations such as people close to a disabled person and/or staff of a supporting agency being informed of support needs, there really isn't a need for others to have information about how a person functions across their daily activities. It isn't necessary or appropriate for people to use these terms casually or socially. Strangers don't need to be provided with information akin to a functioning label. If you are hosting someone and are unsure of the support they will need to attend and participate, default to the guidance given in chapter 1 and extend an invitation to indicate access and accommodation needs. Refrain from asking questions like "What level is he?" or "Is she mild or severe?"

4. Limiting autonomy and applying different standards for behavior

When a disabled person who is no longer a child does things that older people do, it often comes with reactions that would not be applied to nondisabled people. The notion that disabled people curse, sometimes make unsavory choices, and engage in sexual behavior will elicit a gasp from many. In early 2023, a photo of a young woman with Down syndrome smoking a cigarette went viral. It is common for people to either overreact and be appalled by something that typically doesn't rattle them, or underreact and find ways to excuse behavior they would usually take issue with. Both are ableism.

It is important to remember that disabled people deserve the autonomy to make choices about their life. Choosing activities that are at best frowned upon or at worst illegal is part of autonomy. Disabled people are deserving of the full range of options for the human experience, the same as nondisabled people.

Along these lines, assigning exaggerated fragility to disabled people is another way that disabled people can be infantilized. When disabled people are not allowed the opportunity to pursue endeavors simply because they might not succeed, they are being denied aspects of humanity. Hope and disappointment are both experiences that nondisabled people are commonly afforded as a part of life. Success and failure are life's peaks and valleys.

As parents, certainly we sometimes try to shield our kids from disappointment, but as they get older and gain independence, they end up with the autonomy to take the leaps that their parents may have attempted to steer them away from. Disabled people who have less control over their lives sometimes never get these opportunities. And, sometimes, disabled people who do have control over their own lives are still shielded from certain kinds of experiences because of the ableism that tells nondisabled people they are awful if they are part of an experience with a disabled person that doesn't end in what is considered to be a favorable or positive outcome.

Challenge Yourself

Examine your own biases regarding opportunity and choice for disabled adults. Do you cringe at the thought of disabled adults drinking at the bar? Do you consider it inappropriate for a police officer to arrest a disabled person? Would you expect your child to allow a disabled classmate to win at a board game? Take some time to break down these biases so that you can reframe your thinking. You should grant the same freedom, and apply the same level of critical thinking and response, to situations that include disabled people as to those that include the nondisabled.

Bring It Home

I haven't found any children's books that discuss infantilization, but I think most children can relate to the feeling of not wanting to be treated as younger than they are. If you encounter examples of infantilizing or decide to talk to your children about it, you can tell them stories about moments in their life when they have made a push for their own autonomy. As parents, many of us have these stories stored in our memories. I have a video of Pete from when he was three, in which he sternly notifies me that he was "never ever ever ever ever ever going to take a nap again." Kids can easily relate to the feeling of wanting independence and autonomy, and helping them support this natural need and right for people with disabilities is important.

Reinforcing the tendency to look at all people as varying and beautiful in their individuality can lead your children away from infantilization, just as it can lead people away from other forms of ableism. *All the Ways to Be Smart* by Davina Bell and Allison Colpoys walks kids through how individuality makes a society of people who are smart in many different ways. The book mentions a variety of skills that include "tree climbing and slime making, flower picking and finger clicking, finding things on all the pages and sitting still and quiet for ages." The book ends with the following:

> Every hour of every day, we're smart in our own special way.
>   And nobody will ever do . . . the very same smart things
> as you.

9

"DON'T SAY DISABLED"

EUPHEMISMS FOR DISABILITY

And so we have at our disposal a range of linguistic deodorizers, smoke screens, fig leaves. These are euphemisms. They are all about taboos, of course, things that go "bump in the night." They're about politeness. And sometimes they're about skeletons in cupboards.

THESE ARE THE WORDS that Kate Burridge, prominent Australian linguist, used in her 2012 TEDx talk to describe euphemisms. Euphemisms exist because the words they replace are considered taboo by the person saying them. A euphemism is used as a substitute for a word or words "considered to be too harsh or blunt when referring to something unpleasant or embarrassing."

There are many Euphemisms for Disability. They are typically chosen to avoid the words *disability* and *disabled* and include, but are not limited to, to the following:

- Special needs
- Special ed
- Differently abled
- Diffable
- Handi-capable
- Diffability
- Specially abled
- Diversability
- Challenged

The words *disabled* and *disability* are avoided because of the stigma of disability being negative or shameful. When people avoid these terms, it is often because they don't wish to attach the stigma to the person they are talking to or about. I have seen the argument that the word *disability* suggests a lack of ability and that we should focus on what people are able to do, rather than on what they can't do. That explanation sounds well-intentioned, doesn't it? I don't argue that it isn't. That defense clearly comes from a place of wanting to uplift people. But it is rooted in the medical model of disability. If a person thinks that *disabled* means "broken," and they don't want to imply that someone is broken, other words are sought. Dancing around the word *disabled* creates problems for disabled people, though.

On the blog *crippledscholar*, in a November 2017 article called "Euphemisms for Disability Are Infantilizing," the blogger writes:

> I am a 30-year-old woman and I cannot think of a single
> professional setting in which I need to discuss issues pertain-
> ing to my disability such as accommodation where I would
> go into that situation and say, "Hi, I have special needs and
> I need to discuss workplace accommodations." Or "Hi, I'm
> diffabled, who do I talk to about getting speech to text soft-
> ware on my computer?" These terms have no place in a

professional or academic environment. They sound childish and are ultimately confusing.

The disability community claims the word *disabled* and has provided us with a definition of disability that is both clear and respectful. If we reframe the way we think about disability, to recognize that it is not a bad thing and does not mean broken, we will no longer feel the need to avoid these terms. If we listen to disabled voices who are telling us that *disability* isn't a bad word, we can let the euphemisms go.

The word *special* is another word associated with disability that many disabled people don't love. A 2017 video for World Down Syndrome Awareness Day on the YouTube channel CoorDown called "Not Special Needs" beautifully explains why the term *special needs* misses the mark. The narrator of the video, a young woman with Down syndrome, starts the video by reading a report with the headline PEOPLE WITH DOWN SYNDROME HAVE SPECIAL NEEDS. She then ponders the term and goes on to list needs that would meet criteria as being "special." Among other examples, like needing to wear a giant suit of armor or be massaged by a cat, she notes the need to be woken up by a celebrity. In the next scene, actor John C. McGinley enters the room where a woman with Down syndrome is sleeping, leans down close to her, and says "Wakey wakey, eggs and bacey" before the woman sleepily asks, "Who are you?" He goes on to list movies and shows that he has been in before the woman tells him to get out and he says, "My bad," and leaves. The narrator, now surrounded by the four other actors from the skits with Down syndrome, goes on to say, "*That* would be special. But what we really need is education, jobs, and opportunities. Friends, and some love. Just like everybody else. Are these needs special?"

In recent years, the disability community has initiated a discussion regarding the term *special education* as well. Some have proposed that *accessible education* would be more appropriate. I haven't heard of any movements, campaigns, or petitions yet, but I expect there may be some in the years to come. This change would be a larger endeavor, as the term *special education* is used so formally in systems and in legislation.

Rachelle Johnson, a member of the Young Adult Leadership Council of the National Center for Learning Disabilities, wrote an article for the *Office of Special Education and Rehabilitative Services Blog*, which is operated by the US Department of Education. In "Forming a Disability Identity as a Dyslexic," she writes:

> As a child I was diagnosed with dyslexia and attention deficit hyperactivity disorder (ADHD). Adults told me I was "differently abled" and to not categorize myself negatively, as in "disabled." This introduced me to a societal view of "the disabled" and how to navigate an ableist society by distancing from the term disabled. The adults wanted this so I would not be treated in the negative ways people with disabilities often were. I quickly learned how society viewed children with disabilities. I saw differences in how my "disabled versus nondisabled" peers were treated. Other kids made mean remarks because I was pulled out of the room for reading instruction and for the way I read, for which I was embarrassed. I remember a girl teasingly asked, "Why can't you read?" I explained I had dyslexia, a learning disability that made it hard for me to read. She responded laughing, "So you are stupid and disabled?" I tried to repeat what adults had told me: "No, I am 'differently abled,' not disabled like other disabled people," but this explanation failed to make sense to me or the girl teasing me.

Rachelle's story clearly illustrates why some prefer euphemisms for disability. This is because distancing from disability feels very important when disability is viewed to be negative, and your impression is that it will shield you, or your child, from poor treatment. That poor treatment is the product of ableism, and euphemisms are another example of treating one form of ableism with another. Identifying, or being identified, as disabled doesn't change anything about a person, but it can affect access to proper support and accommodation.

Whether dyslexia is a disability is something that I have debated personally, so I am going to share my train of thought for how I reached my own conclusion. As I noted in the introduction to this book, it is not my place to decide for others, and these analyses and conclusions are only mine. I consider Pete, my dyslexic son, to be disabled. He has a learning disability. He needs access to reading and writing instruction appropriate for his neurology and accommodations like dictation and predictive text to support skills like writing and spelling. Dan needs access to braille instruction, equipment, and technology appropriate for his blindness, like braillers; voice-over technology; and accommodations like a scribe or a chance to answer verbally when no brailler is available, to support skills like writing. No one would question that my blind son is disabled, but many people would debate a designation of disability for my dyslexic son, even though they both have needs for access and accommodation to be able to participate and succeed.

Many suggest that dyslexia isn't a disability because if the proper instruction at the proper level of intensity is provided, dyslexics can learn to read and write. The implication is that with the right supports, they no longer face a disadvantage. Isn't that true for everyone with a disability, though? The need for accommodation and access is at the heart of disability, in my opinion, and avoiding a disability designation won't change a person's individual needs.

Certainly, identifying my sons as disabled makes them susceptible to misconceptions and mistreatment, but ableism is the source of those misconceptions and mistreatment—not their disabilities. The word *disabled* doesn't change anything about my boys, but it does help them get the support they require.

In addition to euphemisms, there are other types of sayings and expressions that perpetuate ableism. In a BBC article from April 5, 2021, "The Harmful Ableist Language You Unknowingly Use," author Sara Nović talks about how many common expressions are harmful to the disability community, specifically referencing the expression "falls on deaf ears." Sara writes:

> I like being deaf. I like the silence as well as the rich culture and language deafness affords me. When I see the word "deaf" on the page, it evokes a feeling of pride for my community, and calls to me as if I'm being addressed directly, as if it were my name. So, it always stings when I'm reminded that for many, the word "deaf" has little to do with what I love most—in fact, its connotations are almost exclusively negative.

What Does This Look Like in Action? Manifestations of Euphemisms for Disability

1. Misuse of person-first and identity-first language

When I was in graduate school, we were taught to use person-first language, which suggests that you say "person with a disability" instead of "disabled person." An example is using "person with blindness" instead of "blind person." The push for person-first language came from the idea that disability is only part of a person and not their entire identity.

In recent years, many in the disability community have pushed to transition to identity-first language. If using identity-first language, "autistic person" is preferable to "person with autism." Those who advocate for identity-first language suggest that their disability is part of their identity and not just something they carry around with them. I have heard autistic advocates for identity-first language say things like "Where is my autism? It looks like I left it at home. I guess I am not a person with autism today."

A person's preference between these two is personal and individualistic and neither is right or wrong, though there is often great debate between people who feel strongly for one or the other.

Challenge Yourself

If you have a need to identify a person using either identity-first or person-first language, ask them directly how they identify and would like to be described. "Do you prefer identity-first or person-first language?" I will not tell you whether your default should be identity-first or person-first, if you find yourself in the position of needing to choose. Hopefully, reading the first-person accounts and accessing the resources in this book will help you decide what is right for you. As a person who is asking you to be mindful of individual preferences, I use both in this book.

2. Using disability as a negative metaphor

Like "falls on deaf ears," many of these expressions have made their way into our vocabularies, and most people use them without giving it a second thought. The metaphors I am referencing frame disability as a negative thing. Consider these examples: "turn a blind eye," "tone deaf," "an eye for an eye leaves the whole world blind," and referencing being "crippled with" or "paralyzed by" to mean dominated or troubled by. This also applies to the casual use of mental health related terms, often with the intention of inserting humor. Calling someone "crazy" or "a psychopath" or declaring yourself as bipolar or OCD for dramatic effect are additional examples.

The tendency to use disability in negative expressions is so profound that some terms that were initially used to describe disability are now more known as insults. The term *dumb* initially referred to people who did not speak, and the term *lame* was initially used to denote physical disability. Some suggest that it is now OK to use these words as insults because they are no longer used commonly to refer to disability, but their history matters, and many in the disabled community have identified their continued uses, for any reason, as harmful. The same is true for the *r*-word, which has caused so much harm that it needs to be erased entirely from our vocabularies.

Challenge Yourself

For those of you who are thinking *You can't say anything these days*, allow me to remind you of the vastness of language. There are so many valid ways to make a point because we have so many words to choose from. If you care about growing into someone who wishes to avoid doing harm to disabled people, and desires to lead your children to be anti-ableist, being willing to make the effort to choose alternative, nonableist ways to make your point is a part of that. Instead of "falling on deaf ears," you can say "is not being well received." Instead of "turning a blind eye," you can say "being unwilling to acknowledge." I prefer to use "wild" or "chaotic" instead of "crazy." Why show allegiance to some words and phrases when you can instead show allegiance to making a more accepting existence for disabled people?

3. Terminology blunders

There have been a few times when people are talking about Dan's blindness and uncomfortably trip over their words, trying to figure out what is and is not OK to say. During one conversation with a stranger at the park a few years ago, I found myself debating whether to interrupt the man I was chatting with as he tried out a number of different terms. "Vision . . . sight impaired . . . should I say . . . ." I said, "You can say blind." He seemed relieved. I appreciate that people do not wish to be offensive but have wondered if there might be a less awkward way for uncertain people to determine what terms to use.

Challenge Yourself

You should use accurate terms that are respectful and not out of date. It was clear the man at the park wished to be respectful, so he could have said something like, "Is sight impaired an appropriate term for me to use or do you prefer something else?" This gesture shows respect and a desire to honor personal preferences. This is something you can model for your kids, which will help them learn to be respectful of up-to-date terminology, identity, and individual preference.

If you feel shaky about terminology in general, Emily Ladau offers comprehensive information about disability terminology in her book *Demystifying Disability: What to Do, What to Say, and How to Be an Ally.* After she explains that the term *handicapped* is no longer considered appropriate, she goes on: "Talking about a person? 'Disability' is better than 'handicap.' Pointing out a parking spot with the blue lines? It's 'accessible' parking." Later, she adds more examples of terms that are common in our language but have historically been used to cause harm to people with disabilities and are considered ableist: "Some of the most common examples to look out for include *crazy, dumb, idiot, imbecile, insane, lame, moron, slow,* and *stupid.*"

Bring It Home

When you talk about disability using accurate terms, and don't show signs of discomfort or avoidance of using them, you will be providing an example for your kids that doesn't include euphemisms. This example will send the message that disability isn't taboo or shameful.

When you model asking a close friend or family member what language and terminology they prefer, you teach your kids the importance of defaulting to the person for their individual preferences rather than taking a guess.

The children's book *Just Ask!* by Sonia Sotomayor includes brief explanations of many different disabilities and health conditions, using accurate terms.

> I'm Vijay. I learn about the world differently because I can see, but I can't hear—I'm Deaf. Most of the time I communicate with people using my face and hands through sign language. It's cool to know another language.

Introducing your children to stories about disability, by disabled people, will give them exposure to the ways that people identify and create a sense of comfort surrounding talking about disability appropriately.

10

"DON'T BE SO SENSITIVE"

INVALIDATING DISABILITY

INVALIDATING DISABILITY TELLS US the lie that any objection made by disabled people about their treatment or circumstances is rude, a bid for attention, or an exaggeration. In *Daddy Won't Let Mom Drive the Car*, Jo Elizabeth Pinto shares an instance of invalidation that happened while she was shopping.

> I felt a sudden bump from behind, hard enough to make me stagger. A moment later, someone grasped me by the shoulders and pushed me forward. Then unseen hands scooted my shopping cart away from me.
>
> "Excuse me," I said, partly confused and partly annoyed.
>
> "I need something from the end cap display," a man's voice informed me abruptly. "You're in my way."
>
> "You could have asked me to take a few steps forward," I answered, now much more annoyed than confused. "I didn't appreciate you touching me without permission. A simple excuse me would have done just fine."

"But you're blind."

"True enough," I nodded. "My eyes don't work, but my ears do, and so do my feet. I'm not a piece of furniture you can move around at your convenience."

"You seem really angry. I guess you're having a bad day."

I didn't dignify that comment with an answer. I had been having a perfectly good day till I got shoved out of the way like an old suitcase. But explaining that to the person who does the shoving makes no difference most of the time. It's unacceptable for a man in our society to put his hands on a woman without a disability for any reason, except perhaps if he's saving her from imminent danger. Add a disability to the equation, though, and all bets are off. He's just trying to help, he doesn't know any better, he feels awkward and isn't sure how to start a conversation—any of these excuses are accepted as viable. If the disabled woman protests, she's considered angry, bitter, or bitchy.

Invalidating Disability also shows up when a disabled person's advocacy for access, accommodation, and support is called into question. In a July 2020 article called "The Burden and Consequences of Self-Advocacy for Disabled BIPOC," written for the Disability Visibility Project, Aparna R, a writer, disability activist, public researcher, and grad student, wrote:

As someone with chronic illnesses and invisible disabilities, and as an Indian American woman from a culture in which disability as a concept is taboo—a word hushed into silence if spoken aloud, I was years into adulthood before I realized disability was an identity I had the right to claim. It was even longer before I learned about the decades long history of Disability Rights activists, including disabled BIPOC (Black, Indigenous, People of Color), in the

US. Their work paved the way for me and allowed me to take pride in a community and identity I had been taught was shameful. Without owning this identity, I could not see how ableist oppression was systemic and that it needed to be pushed back. Every denial of accommodations, every dismissal of me and my needs, every time an instructor or employer thought I was too "difficult," "unreasonable," or "too burdensome," to accommodate were not instances of individual bad actors, but part of a wider pattern of ableist oppression.

It is widely reported that requests for accommodations and access for disabled people are often ignored or left unfulfilled. We have been working to help Dan understand ableism so that he will be equipped to advocate for himself. He had a beautiful advocacy experience during his second-grade year that, thankfully, ended with a positive result. His school district introduced coding in kindergarten, and Dan had previous coding experience with materials that were accessible or made so by staff (including a fabric coding map that his para sewed to make it tactile.) In second grade, though, the software became inaccessible. Dan's para supported him in writing a letter in braille and encouraged him to take it to his principal. The letter said:

> Dear Principle W. I am sad and frustrated today. My class is coding but I can't do anything. I have a cool program called Code Jumper but it needs a laptop with bluetooth I can connect to it. My teachers have asked for a laptop that I can do this but nothing has happened. I have learned all I can about the coding pieces. Now I want to start coding! Can you please help me get what I need?

His principal could have responded in a number of different ways. He could have been dismissive and suggested that coding is supplemental and there are alternative activities Dan could do instead. He could have been defensive and pointed out other adaptive equipment and technologies that had been purchased to provide Dan with access. He could have passively acknowledged it and made an empty promise to remedy the situation without taking any additional action. Instead, he immediately ordered a laptop and then called me. He told me that what happened with Dan was one of the most impactful experiences that he had yet had as a school principal of many years and admitted that it was problematic that Dan had to advocate for himself, indicating that he was embarrassed that access hadn't already been provided. Dan has been coding since.

Other than access having been provided in the first place, this is an ideal outcome, and we are grateful that Dan has school staff who support both access and advocacy. I also appreciated that his principal acknowledged the initial failing on the school's part, especially because he followed it up with action to make it right. An openness to see accessibility failings, rather than being defensive or dismissive, is an important piece of moving in the right direction.

When someone's needs aren't supported the way that they were for Dan, though, the impact can be harmful. Our journey with navigating Pete's learning disability gave me a front-row seat to the toll that invalidation can take on a child. It was often suggested that Pete was not asserting himself, needed more incentive, or simply needed us to make it clear to him what was expected. I watched my normally happy and somewhat carefree boy transition to a state of perpetual stress, defensiveness, and frustration. Once we found out about his learning disability, accommodations entered the discussion, but there was still often a degree of pushback and questioning regarding whether he really needed them. These experiences created very negative feelings about school that have taken Pete a while to recover from.

In a November 2022 episode on the *Stuttering Foundation Podcast*, Christopher Anderson talked to host Sara MacIntyre about his book *Every Waking Moment* and the emotional effects of stuttering that were unaddressed for much of his life.

> That is exactly my aim . . . to highlight how each moment impacts us from the start. You think about our formative years and how stuttering impacts them. If you break down a moment of stuttering, you move through the anxiety and anticipation, the fear as it onsets, the wanting to escape amidst it and then afterwards, the shame, all the thoughts, the exhaustion. You do that for years, through childhood, and the thing that I knew all along is that I never had any help with how to handle that. I knew that, as a kid, . . . the only thing ever worked on was how my speech sounded. I wanted to get out of my head. I wanted to be more social, I just didn't know how to get over the experience that I felt inside. That's part of the reason that I walk through that in the book, because I want to bring more focus on that inner experience.

Providing support for certain aspects of a disability while ignoring others is an example of invalidation, and in Christopher Anderson's case, the emotional distress that he faced was overlooked while much energy was spent on efforts that reinforced it.

In a May 2021 article for The Mighty, "How Ableism Affects the Mental Health of Disabled People," disabled contributor Kelly Douglas writes:

> Studies have shown that 17.4 percent of people with disabilities experience "frequent mental distress"—a higher percentage than in the able-bodied, neurotypical population.

Additionally, depression symptoms are two to 10 times more common in people with disabilities, and higher levels of anxiety have been reported in people with disabilities as well. While some may attribute these mental illnesses to frustration with physical limitations, this high prevalence of anxiety and depression is more often related to how society *views*, *treats* and *excludes* people with disabilities rather than to disability symptoms themselves. . . .

The ableism I faced as a child with mild cerebral palsy, from doctors constantly focusing on my body's weaknesses to facing non-consensual surgeries that were meant to "fix" my body to the pressure I faced to hide my disability by any means possible significantly affected my mindset later in life. By the time I was a teenager, I was struggling with anxiety from constantly concealing my cerebral palsy, and in college, the pressure to "surpass" my disability contributed to depression, suicidality, and an eating disorder.

The impacts ableism can have sometimes lead people to try hard to hide their disability, and this is another way that Invalidating Disability shows up. In *Disability Visibility*, Sapora Ariel wrote a chapter called "Selma Blair Became a Disabled Icon Overnight. Here's Why We Need More Stories Like Hers." Sapora writes about Selma Blair's red-carpet appearance at the 2019 Vanity Fair awards:

In her first public appearance since publicly disclosing her multiple sclerosis (MS) diagnosis, Blair instantly became a disabled icon. As the camera's bright lights flash around her, Blair was the image of elegance. I watched her with her head held high, her cape flowing around her, her cane in hand, and meeting the camera with her eyes, perfectly posed. Then, as if breaking character, she stopped posing, took a step back, and her face crinkled slightly as she began to cry. Her manager, Troy Nankin, came over to her and helped wipe her tears. She held on to his arm while she gathered herself, saying, "It just took so much to get out." There I was, a disabled woman in her mid-twenties, living in my parents' house in Maine, in flannel pajamas and slippers, not a speck of makeup on my face, my thinning hair held back in a headscarf, with my $12 cane I'd gotten off of Amazon, watching her on my laptop. There she was: blond hair, slicked back, a stunning gown with solid sweeping lines, offset by the drama of the sheer cape, a real damned diamond on her cane, her perfect makeup somehow flawless even after wiping away tears, surrounded by photographers calling her name—and yet in that tiny moment, I felt I could relate to what she was feeling. *It just took so much to get out.*

So often, celebrities and people in the public eye go to great lengths to conceal their disabilities. Without the kind of visibility that happens when a celebrity such as Selma Blair shows up even when her disability cannot be concealed, people with disabilities sometimes feel as if the extra effort that is required to exist as disabled in the world goes unnoticed or minimized. When disability is hidden away, the realities of disability are as well, which contributes to misconceptions.

Sometimes, Invalidating Disability happens in an attempt to "normalize" whatever is being reported, with the impression that it being "normalized" will make it less problematic for the person reporting the challenge. This is a common experience for those the autistic community. When disclosing their diagnosis, many report hearing the phrase "We're all a little bit autistic." In a January 2021 article for *Forbes* called "Is Everyone a Little Autistic?" Nancy Doyle writes:

Unbeknownst to the people who say it, it is actually a very controversial statement. To people who have experienced being othered and ostracized for their differences it sounds flippant and minimizes our experiences. If everyone was a little Dyslexic, Dyspraxic, Autistic or ADHD then why would neurominorities experience the exclusion that they do? It's a little bit like saying to someone with chronic cluster migraines that "we all have headaches, don't we?" And the answer is no, we don't all have headaches like that.

Neurominorities have been empowered through the neurodiversity movement. We have gained self-confidence and ownership of our identities through accepting that our brains are different and that that difference is okay. So, when someone who has not experienced any great hardships due to their more balanced cognitive abilities tries to claim that they are "a little bit Autistic" it is not surprising that we feel they are incorrectly trying to claim a piece of our hard won identity.

What Does This Look Like in Action? Manifestations of Invalidating Disability

1. Denying or minimizing ableist encounters and getting defensive

Jo Elizabeth Pinto's story is an example of this manifestation. She was mistreated by the person who took no accountability and invalidated her attempts to correct him. He also gaslighted her for her feelings about being treated poorly.

Challenge Yourself

If a person tells you that something you have done or said is ableist, it can lead to bewilderment and/or defensiveness. If you allow yourself to be open to what the person is telling you, you put yourself in the position of learning and growing. Arguing with the person about whether what you did was ableist suggests that you are the expert and have the ability to perceive the other person's experience. You are the expert on yourself, and though perhaps your intention was pure, clearly the impact of whatever happened did not match. In these cases, simple accountability, paired with commitment to do better, is powerful.

Try not to go on and on about your mistake, though. I have done this before and later realized that I was making more work for the person I was over-apologizing to. Many disabled people have indicated that the energy they need to muster to even point out ableism is taxing. When you over-apologize, it creates a need for them to expend more energy to respond to you, whether it be to excuse you, to ask you to stop carrying on about it, or to console you. In any case, it is extra energy, not helpful, and now centers you rather than the ableism. Something along the lines of "I'm sorry for my misstep. Thank you for pointing it out" is sufficient.

2. Denying or downplaying challenges related to disability

There are many disabling conditions that do not have visible evidence, and often disabled people who can conceal their disability choose to do so. The reasons for that are personal and likely vary from person to person, but it can be assumed that ableism and stigma contribute to why people choose to conceal disability. They find themselves with the choice to either reveal their disability and face stigma or conceal a part of their identity. Often, people with invisible disabilities don't make an effort to conceal their disability, but manifestations of their disability are noticed and then judged or ostracized.

The stats related to what percentage of disabilities are invisible seem to be highly variable, from 10 to 95 percent. Given that the most recent report from the Centers for Disease Control and Prevention notes sixty-one million people living with disability, the most conservative counts still indicate millions of people in the United States alone have disabilities that cannot be observed or determined at a glance. Though there may be advantages to a person's disability status being undetected, there are major challenges as well.

In an article for Medium by Stephanie Barnes called "Suffering in Silence: The Epidemic of Invisible Disabilities in the Workplace," a thorough but nonexhaustive list of invisible disabilities is given.

> Some common invisible disabilities include psychiatric disorders such as depression, post-traumatic stress (PTSD), anxiety, bipolar, and schizophrenia as well as autism spectrum disorder (ASD), learning disabilities, attention-deficit hyperactivity disorder (ADHD), diabetes, chronic fatigue syndrome, cystic fibrosis, chronic pain, epilepsy, cancer and HIV/AIDS. All of these conditions can limit a person's everyday activities, senses or movements.

The article speaks to the possible reasons people choose to hide their disabilities and cites the possibility of discrimination, the Presumption of Incompetence, and disability misconceptions. Basically, people mostly choose to hide their disabilities because of the forms of ableism we are talking about here.

In an article on the website Bored Panda from January 2023, Jurgita Dominauskaitė and Monika Pašukonytė recount the story of a family who faced criticism from extended family members for an accommodation they created for their six-year-old daughter. The arti-cle shares that their foster daughter has a need for a safe place when feeling overwhelmed, so the family put up a tent in their living room that was designated as her space. Their daughter previously would hide when becoming overwhelmed, and they often could not find her. Their daughter's tent was her space, and no one was allowed inside without her permission. Extended family members took issue when their daughter had toys inside that the other children were not allowed to play with. These family members minimized the needs of the little girl and determined that her parents were indulging her selfishness, rather than understanding that it was a necessary accommodation to create safety for her. This story is very familiar to family members and caregivers of disabled children. When your child's needs require action that does not look the same as the ways most other children's needs are met, it is very common for misunderstandings to take place. I often hear stories about encounters in grocery stores that involve a judgmental stranger declaring that a child with an invisible disability in crisis is being spoiled by their parent, when in reality the parent knows what she needs in the moment and is acting accordingly.

In these cases, the distinction between equality and equity comes to mind. Equality is everyone getting the same thing, whereas equity is everyone getting what they need. Though this can be challenging to explain to children, I have seen that it is possible. I have never seen a child get upset that they don't get to use a cane when it is explained why Dan uses one. "He needs this to be able to get around safely. You don't need one because you can use your eyes to see the information that he gets from the cane."

Challenge Yourself

Understand that disability is complex and that you cannot easily deter-mine a person's disability status by looking at them. Though instances of people faking disability do happen, they are extremely rare, and you should not use these instances as justification to question someone's disability designation.

If you think you know what is best for someone else's child without knowing their whole story or having all of the background and experiences, lean into humility. Think of all the things you know about your own children that strangers wouldn't know. Consider how you might know what they are thinking in a given situation and remember situations where others may have misunderstood them. Add to these considerations the fact that disability brings complexity that you might not have the experience to understand. What your kids have needed in certain moments doesn't have anything to do with what other kids might need. Understanding the importance of people getting what they actually need instead of what everyone else gets is vital to appropriate and adequate inclusion efforts.

3. Dismissing complex feelings disabled people have about their experiences

Disability can cause complex feelings in disabled people for a number of reasons. Challenges related to these feelings being overlooked or dismissed is another manifestation of Invalidating Disability. Whether it is due to a person struggling with feelings about the ways in which their disability affects their functioning; the emotional fallout of the judgment, pity, mocking, shame, and other mistreatment that ableism perpetuates; or feelings of frustration and defeat related to being denied access and accommodation, being disabled can bring feelings that nondisabled people won't fully understand.

Challenge Yourself

If you are the sympathetic ear for a disabled friend or family member, try to avoid minimizing feelings related to the challenges they face. If someone around you is struggling, whether they are disabled or not, default to compassion and kindness. If you are close to a disabled person, let them know that you desire to support them in all the ways that are helpful and make sure they know that they can talk to you about things that seem difficult. You don't need to go out of your way to point out things *you* think might make their life harder, as that can be awkward, uncomfortable, and presumptuous. Let them initiate and lead the discussion.

4. Attempting to relate to disability-related experiences as a nondisabled person

Another way that invalidating manifests is when a nondisabled person responds to a challenging factor of a person's disability by attempting to relate to it. This seems to be a common phenomenon in parenting. When a parent shares something happening with their child that seems hard, the other parent often tries to make them feel less alone by saying, "Oh yeah, my kid does that too." Sometimes, the situations are equally matched and this is an act of solidarity. Other times, though, when a challenge is unique to a particular circumstance, like a disability, that gesture can feel like invalidation. "We're all a little autistic" applies here.

Challenge Yourself

Instead of trying to make a person feel less shame about a barrier connected to their disability by trying to relate to it, consider if your energy might be better spent in efforts to support access and accommodation that might reduce or eliminate the barrier. And if it is an uncompromising barrier, try to reframe your interpretation of what your role is. Instead of assuming that your role is to minimize the feelings you expect the person is having, even if it is with good intentions, consider instead a role of present neutrality. There is great power in a simple check-in: "How are you feeling about it?" or "Do you want to talk about it?"

Bring It Home

Though it is important to lead our kids away from assuming deficit in people with disabilities, it is equally important to teach them to trust disabled people when they relay their experiences and barriers. The understanding that every circumstance comes with unique triumphs and challenges is an important one to accept and pass along. The children's book *Drawn to Be You* by Corey Landreth, Andrea Landreth, and Jefferson Knapp is about a young man named Trent, who is the book's illustrator.

> His name is Trent and just like you
> He enjoys doing things that are fun.
> He loves music, cartoons and swimming,
> But drawing will always be #1!
> He's unable to talk like other people,
> It's tough saying what's on his mind.
> And when people try to speak with him,
> A sentence is hard to find.

It isn't taboo to talk about struggle if the struggle is relayed by the disabled person. The problem comes when we assume the feelings, struggles, competencies, and capabilities. Modeling this distinction, between assumption and actual relayed experiences, for our children will help them become supportive to those with disabilities in their lives.

11

"WERE YOU BORN LIKE THAT?"

DISREGARD OF PRIVATE INFORMATION IN DISABILITY

IMAGINE THIS SCENARIO: You are in line at the grocery store and the person in line ahead of you turns around and notices you. He visually studies you for a moment and then says, "I see you have facial hair. How old were you when you went through puberty, and when did your facial hair start to grow?" How would you rate the appropriateness of that question, in that setting, given your relationship? Would you consider it invasive?

This scenario probably seems unlikely to most, but for people with disabilities, these kinds of interactions are quite common. The Disregard of Private Information in Disability tells us that we are entitled to the private information of strangers if they have a visible disability. A friend told me that he was once approached by someone who said, "I'm a biology major and am wondering why you are blind." He

emphasized the absence of even a simple greeting or introduction—
"Not even a hi or hello."

Activist Stella Young, introduced earlier, wrote the following in
an article called "The Wheel Perspective" in March 2012:

> It doesn't matter how we got like this. Really. Are you ask-
> ing because you want to know or because you need to? If
> you're just sitting next to one of us on the train, or taking
> our order at a cafe, you don't actually need to know. If we've
> actually met and have had a conversation beyond "Do you
> want honey with your chai?" then perhaps it gets a little
> more relevant. It might come up in conversation, and when
> it does, we'll be happy to tell you. It's just not a very good
> opening line.

On her website Fashionably Ill, in an article titled "Stop Asking
Disabled People 'What Happened to You?'" Jessica Gimeno writes:

> You may think your question is innocuous but do you real-
> ize you are the ninth person to ask that question this week,
> maybe even today? Imagine waking up tired every day and
> living with 24/7 pain. You have to choose between eating
> lunch or taking a shower because of limited energy. Then,
> imagine trying to get somewhere knowing it might take you
> twice as long as your able-bodied peers and that you will be
> bombarded by strangers asking, "What happened to you?"
> Now, do this every time you leave the house.
>
> Disabled people are not museum exhibits. We don't owe
> strangers and curious people our time and energy. For all
> the times we explain why we look this way or why we are
> using mobility aids, we are not being paid for our time. I
> have one friend who says that she likes it when people ask

her, "What's wrong with you?" because she views it as a teachable moment. But I ain't Oprah.

If grown adults are compelled to ask personal questions about disabled people, then we shouldn't be surprised that it is also common for children. In *Demystifying Disability*, Emily Ladau shares that she is generally open to questions from children but that not all disabled people are. She talks about situations when children ask questions in ways that are potentially offensive, for example, a child asking, "What is wrong with your legs?" She says she personally would respond by explaining that she was born with something called a disability. She shares a story about when she and her family took her young neighbor to a movie and the child asked a ticket taker with a facial difference "What happened to your face?" She explains how she talked to the child after.

> I resisted the urge to scold my neighbor, instead guiding her to thank the ticket-taker for answering her question. As we headed to the theater, I grappled with what to say. I guess I subconsciously assumed that since my neighbor was so familiar with my mother and me using wheelchairs, she'd be just as comfortable with other physical differences. It was a valuable lesson for us both. I tried to explain that no one looks the same and that it's one of the things that makes the world such a beautiful place. I tried to tell her that it's okay to be curious but it's not nice to just shout out questions. Honestly, I struggled to find the right words. But she seemed to understand, in her own eight-year-old way, that difference isn't a bad thing.

When I first became Dan's mom, I didn't really see much of a problem with people asking these kinds of questions. I hadn't yet started listening to the voices of disabled adults and was interacting with the world with only the experiences and perspectives I had acquired as a person who, at that time, identified as neurotypical and nondisabled. As a result, I usually cheerfully and eagerly answered these questions. Even when people would sometimes say, "Feel free to tell me it's none of my business," I would usually respond with something like, "Oh no! I like to talk about it." I was operating under the belief that disability is not shameful to talk about and thought the education I was providing would be helpful.

I was not considering, though, that I was sharing information that is not mine to share. In those moments, I also modeled for Dan that strangers were entitled to his story, his medical history, and his privacy. I reinforced this form of ableism in every interaction when someone asked and, unbeknownst to me, fed a dynamic that will make it less likely that disabled people will be entitled to their privacy. Dan and I have had many discussions since, and I am trying to undo the precedent that I set and make sure Dan knows that he is entitled to his privacy and doesn't owe anyone information that he does not want to share. When we know better, we do better. I am still figuring out how to navigate what stories are mine to share, as a parent, and what stories belong to my kids. I ask their permission before sharing anything about them but sometimes still struggle with determining which things I shouldn't even ask to share.

What Does This Look Like in Action? Manifestations of the Disregard of Private Information in Disability

1. Asking strangers for medical information

Asking for private health information from someone, outside of personal and intimate relationships, is an example of this form of ableism. Perhaps because some disabilities can be observed physically, the impression is that all related information is up for public access. This notion is false. If you are a stranger and are asking about details of a person's disability, like "How long have you been like that?" or "Can you see/hear/walk at all?" you are placing an expectation for that person to give you their private information.

Challenge Yourself

Remember that you can make small talk with disabled people about the same things that you talk about with nondisabled people. If you can refrain from asking nondisabled people for private health information, then you can do the same when interacting with disabled people.

As stated by Stella Young previously, if you don't have a relationship deeper than acquaintance, then you don't need to know the other person's private information. When talking to your kids, it is important to make the distinction between what is and is not our business to know. Explain the difference between "Where did you get those cool shoes?" and "What happened to your legs?" Help your children understand how being asked about something very private and personal by a stranger might feel uncomfortable. This, of course, is a conversation that will have to align with your child's developmental stage and consequent abilities. Children are children and these questions might still happen, and that doesn't mean you need to feel shame about it. You can use these instances as teachable moments that will most likely prove to be meaningful for learning and future interactions.

2. Casually talking about a person's disability without their participation

Talking about a person's disability because it is automatically disclosed via being visibly observed, without the person being involved in the conversation, is a manifestation of this form of ableism. Whether in the break room at work, on the sidelines at a game, in a classroom, or during a medical appointment, engaging in this behavior is almost always inappropriate. It feels much better to be talked *to* than talked *about*; casual chats about someone's personal aspects can feel like a violation of their dignity, regardless of whether what is being said is good or bad. A discussion related to necessary access or accommodations that is simply being relayed, with the disabled person's consent, is an example of an exception.

Because of his disability, it is common for other parents to ask me questions about Dan when he is with me. Even though this might be common practice, it seems important to remedy, because Dan will someday be an adult. If he grows up used to this dynamic, he might not feel empowered to speak up later when he is being talked about instead of talked to, which we learned in chapter 1 is common for disabled adults. If we can empower disabled children by setting the precedent that they should be talked to and not about, it might make self-advocacy easier for them as they get older.

Challenge Yourself

When it comes to adults, I can't think of any instances when a casual conversation about their disability without them being present might occur out of necessity or be appropriate. When it comes to kids, though, sometimes these kinds of conversations are necessary for care or support. Before discussing a child who is nearby, it is respectful to tell the child, "I am going to talk to so-and-so right now about x because of y." This might be appropriate if the child doesn't seem interested in the conversation but you know he might overhear and will be able to tell he is being talked about. Another option is to loop in the child as you talk: "We have been doing x, and he seems to be having fun. Is that right, [child]? Are you having fun when we do that?"

If your child asks about the observable difference in a trusted friend or family member who is disabled, it is probably OK to share a few basic facts to answer their questions. If they ask questions that are more in-depth and personal, like about the feelings of the disabled person, consider answering that you cannot speak to the personal feelings and experiences of another person and suggest that they ask the friend/family member directly. This not only sends the message that the disabled person is the expert of their own experience but also gives your child the opportunity to come up with appropriate questions with your help and support.

3. Expecting a disabled person to educate you about disability

Asking a disabled person many questions about their disability places an expectation on them to educate you. Outside the context of organic and consensual conversations in personal relationships, when you expect a disabled person to educate you on the details of their disability, not only are you violating their right to privacy, but you are also adding another task to their plate.

Challenge Yourself

When it comes to learning general facts about conditions of disability, education can happen on your own time. Disabled people write memoirs and articles; they maintain social media accounts and host podcasts. Those resources, along with general information you can find at the library and online, can provide answers to your basic questions. It is your responsibility to dedicate time to seek out and learn from these available sources.

If your child is wondering about what disability a person might have, you can explain to them that *some* strangers they meet might be OK with answering questions. You can help them figure out how to ask the person if they are interested in answering a question so that they are respectful. Make sure to prepare them for the fact that some people might not be interested in talking about it. For example, "I was wondering if I can ask you a question about your disability so that I can learn more about it, but I understand if you don't feel like it."

4. Expecting the disabled person in your group to present on disability

It is not uncommon for disabled people to be asked to do group presentations for the purpose of educating others in the group about their disability. This can happen in places of employment, classrooms, church groups, parent groups, and just about any other place where groups of people gather on a regular basis. Just as nothing else is universal, how the person being asked to do this will feel is highly variable. I'm certain that some people do not feel burdened and have interest in doing this sort of thing, but that doesn't mean you should disregard the value of their time. And others might not be interested in providing education or the privacy and vulnerability aspects that come with it.

Challenge Yourself

If you are in charge of a group and considering asking a disabled person in the group to give their time for the purpose of educating, consider making compensation part of that ask. You can leave it up to the person by asking what kind of compensation they would require, if they are interested. If you are on a limited budget, you can make an offer based on the resources you have available while also conveying that the person will not be penalized for declining.

Asking disabled children to do Q&A is also something that should be given careful thought and consideration. Dan's classmates have been educated about the aspects of his disability unfamiliar to them in a variety of ways. We know that new classmates will have questions, and we do not want Dan to be constantly burdened by them. I prefer the idea of children being educated about disability on an ongoing basis so that when they have a disabled child in their class, it will not be novel to them. Though Dan had a few spiels that he would give when asked specific questions and did a beginning-of-the-year Q&A a few times, I'm fairly certain he spends the first few months of every new school year talking quite a bit about his blindness, regardless of whether we plan any sort of class-wide info session. I still haven't figured out what the answer is, but my hope is that better education will make some sort of positive difference.

For this reason, I am a fan of educational institutions having staff dedicated to diversity, equity, and inclusion who can ensure that disability education is part of what children are learning in school. This will take at least some of the burden of education off disabled children themselves and their caregivers. The same can be said for companies that make inclusion a priority, as it can be an actionable step toward combating ableism in the workplace and eliminating what disabled employees will have to shoulder otherwise.

Bring It Home

When it comes to acquiring information about disability, many factors affect what is appropriate or considerate. Here is a summary of things to consider.

1. Educate yourself as much as you can using publicly available resources.
2. Your relationship to a person is a key factor in determining how appropriate, or inappropriate, it is for you to ask a question.
3. If it feels right to ask a stranger a personal question, be mindful of how you ask and be accepting if the person declines.

Disability education is an ongoing process, as there are countless disabilities and human conditions that your kids haven't already had experience with. If you discover there is a student in your child's class who is disabled or has a specific medical condition, taking some time to learn more about that condition is a great way to help your child be a supportive classmate. When one of my boys came home explaining that he had a classmate with diabetes, we spent time learning more about diabetes so that I would have the opportunity to answer questions that he otherwise might ask his classmate. Some questions can be answered with general information that can easily be found, whereas other questions must be answered by the person themself.

A multitude of children's books teach about specific disabilities. For example, in *Lee, the Rabbit with Epilepsy* by Deborah M. Moss, Lee's doctor explains to him what epilepsy is:

> "When you have epilepsy, your brain sometimes sends out mixed-up messages so you can't move, or think, or do things quite right for a little while. That's called having a seizure." Lee wrinkled her forehead. "I'm mixed up right now. Does that mean I'm having a seizure?"

Dr. Bob answers Lee's question and goes on to explain, "There are different kinds of seizures, too. Some seizures make you fall down and shake all over. Some seizures make just one arm or leg shake. And other seizures make everything look or sound strange to you for a moment."

My Life with Blindness by Mari Schuh is written from experiences shared by Kadence, a blind student from the Minnesota State Academy for the Blind: "I read large print words because I can't see smaller words. Sometimes I listen to audiobooks. I also read braille.

Braille letters and words are made of raised dots. I feel the dots with my fingertips."

These books, and books like them, have already done the work of explaining specific disabilities in kid-friendly terms. Truth be told, I find myself learning a lot from these types of books, too. You don't have to wait until you know of a specific disability in your child's sphere to start educating them, either. You can slowly add to your child's disability repertoire by continuing to educate. Chances are, they will access and apply what they learn at some point.

Everybody Has Something is a book my friend Margaret Domnick wrote after her son was diagnosed with a liver disorder. In it, she begins to describe his condition in simple terms: "Hi, I'm Jack. And guess what? I have something. My mom says that everybody has something. Sometimes you can see it. Sometimes you can't."

The book goes on to highlight a variety of differences across a variety of children. Books like this increase awareness not only about the many aspects of individuality but also about the reader's individuality and how that individuality connects us to others with their own somethings.

Providing general education about disabilities is also important, and there are resources out there for kids that do this beautifully. These kinds of resources provide information that can be applied to many people children encounter and will support their understanding on a larger scale. Books like *A Kids Book About Disabilities* by Kristine Napper are helpful, offering perspectives like the following:

> If you have a question about me, my chair, or my disability, it's OK to ask. Most of the time, it's totally OK! But some questions aren't nice. Some are kind of mean. Questions like . . . "What's wrong with you?" "How do you use the bathroom?" "What happened to you?" "Can you have babies?"

Not So Different: What You Really Want to Ask About Having a Disability by Shane Burcaw is another book that offers general information from the perspective of a disabled person. Often, these books provide both education about disability and practical information about what you can do if you have questions.

12

"I DON'T THINK OF YOU
AS DISABLED"

ERASURE OF DISABILITY

IN THE 1911 NOVEL *The Secret Garden* by Frances Hodgson Burnett, one of the primary complications of the story is a main character's rejection by his father, largely because the son is disabled. In the final chapter, the father returns from a long trip to find his son out of bed, outdoors, "healthy looking" and walking. The book ends with the father and son walking together in the beloved garden.

> Across the lawn came the Master of Misselthwaite and he looked as many of them had never seen him. And by his side, with his head up in the air and his eyes full of laughter walked as strongly and steadily as any boy in Yorkshire—Master Colin!

More than a century later, our feel-good "disability, be gone!" stories come in the form of online videos and news stories that reveal the moment that disability was seemingly erased. A high school graduate stands from his wheelchair and takes a few steps across the stage. A deaf child's cochlear implant is turned on, and the child responds to sound for all to see. The tears are instant, and there is joy and relief. The feelings these stories and videos evoke largely come from Erasure of Disability, which essentially is the passive-aggressive alternative to Disability as a Deficit. Erasure doesn't say that disability is bad but, rather, goes out of its way to point out that the absence of disability is ideal. When the way a person exists in the world is outside the norm, the prevalent response has been to modify the person to make them "normal." This occurs outside of disability as well, but is a very common, pervasive, and damaging practice for the disability community.

In an article on Medium called "Stop Sharing Those Feel-Good Cochlear Implant Videos," originally from the *Establishment*, University of Southern California disability specialist and accessibility consultant Morgan Leahy writes:

> The issue is that when people view these activation videos as tear-jerking material of disabled people being "cured," it perpetuates many foundations of ableism. For some members of the Deaf community, glamorizing and celebrating cochlear implants this way amounts to saying "your existence is impaired and diminished and needs to be fixed for you to have a full life."

It isn't just the absence of disability that erasure highlights. Erasure of Disability also factors into how we frame and exalt independence. Erasure of Disability won't tell you that utilizing support is bad, but it will glorify accomplishments made without support. For many in the disability community, support workers are key in the actualization of their independence. In *Year of the Tiger*, Alice Wong talks about independence.

I think people with disabilities who have similar conditions, we all realize that what is normal is on a continuum, and so is my functioning and my independence. It means it's very fluid. People think independence means being able to do everything yourself, by yourself. That's one way to look at it. Another way is to say, "As long as I can direct my own services and direct my own care, I am still independent." . . . That, to me, is the essence of what it means to be independent—a person that is exercising their autonomy to make their choices and take risks.

Erasure of Disability also factors into productivity and the worth that is often attached to what, and how much, a person produces. Disabled people being discounted and discarded because of issues related to productivity, and inflexible productivity standards, are examples of this manifestation.

In an article posted on the website for the Petrie-Flom Center at Harvard Law, "Injustice Anywhere: The Need to Decouple Disability and Productivity," staff member Brooke Ellison writes:

Throughout the 17th century, when the age of colonialism brought the ravages of disease and treacherous conditions, thereby creating a wide variation in body morphology, less attention was paid to bodily norms, and significant attention was paid to the ability one had to contribute to productivity and providing for the community. That characteristic, much more than any physical one, denoted disability.

For centuries since then, the image of disability in the U.S. has been contextualized in just these terms: it is not simply a physical or mental status that designates "disability," per se, but also how this status implicates one's ability to produce. This mercantilistic, utilitarian view of disability and of humanity has had immeasurable consequences on how we have come to value—or fail to value—disabled people's lives and their contributions to the economy.

In an article for Medium, "What Does It Mean to Be 'Productive'? A Conversation Between Disability Allies," two occupational therapists working in disability academia, Susan Mahipaul and Erika Katzman, discuss challenges related to productivity standards in academic professions. They explicitly discuss the intersections and differences between their experiences—Susan is disabled and Erika is nondisabled. Susan shares that, on a good day, she can muster three to four hours of productive work, as much of her day is consumed with tasks to manage her health conditions, including physiotherapy and medications that affect her ability to function. Erika responds:

> Our mornings look different, but the way I see it, you also wake up and dive into work—it's just that the work we do at some points in our days is not seen and valued equally in this world. The writing and lecture prep that fills my mornings are seen to be more valuable than the time you spend keeping your body well. If we understood the time you spent keeping your body/mind well as disability work, our days wouldn't look so different.

Susan then says:

> When you describe my three- to four-hour workdays as equitable, I feel buoyed. It's one of the most supportive things that anyone has ever said to me and helps me to challenge internalized feelings of inadequacy; like, I'm expected to fit all of my personal care in and still work eight-hour days. I do manage to fit an awful lot in.

Erasure of Disability can cause complex feelings in disabled people, as it can sometimes lead them to strive to reduce aids and supports
that signal the presence of disability or to push their bodies beyond
their limits. In *Have Dog, Will Travel*, Stephen Kuusisto talks about
how he had gone well into adulthood without using any orientation
and mobility tools simply because he had grown up being told to hide
his blindness. After almost four decades of life, he decided to become
a guide dog user and completed guide dog training.

> My mother still didn't like my embrace of blindness. Now
> that graduation was coming I called her to share how good
> the training experience had been. I talked about [guide dog]
> Corky, told her how Corky had taken me through the Wal-
> dorf. I said she was slowly working her way into my bed at
> night. "In Corky's works the bed is the sign of justice," I told
> my mother. Then she said it: "I wish you weren't doing this.
> Now everyone will know you can't see . . ."
>
> I was never going to change her. And when all was
> said and done it wasn't my job. My job (so to speak) was to
> travel with Corky, forgetting old fantasies about mind over
> matter, to forget my mother's insistence that not thinking
> about disability would make it vanish.

In a post written in January 2019 on the blog *homo qui vixit*,
a blogger known as endever* who identifies as trans and autistic,
discusses how speaking with one's mouth is prioritized over other
forms of communication and tells of their own personal experience
with augmentative and alternative forms of communication, or AAC.

> It also did not seem to occur to anybody that speech might
> be even more difficult for me than was represented in
> my actual output, and that it was just getting more and

more exhausting the more I tried to say things the way they wanted me to. It's only now, as an adult, that having access to AAC is showing me how different my early life could have been if that struggle had been better recognized. With AAC it's like a giant weight I hadn't fully realized was there has been lifted. For example, in sign language I find myself outgoing and energized by social interaction, the complete opposite of my other experiences socializing. Using dedicated high tech AAC on a day to day basis tangibly improves my life as I can express myself more fully with less difficulty and I have more energy to spend on other tasks. So why didn't anyone try me out on these options when I was in speech therapy?

Am I a speech-language pathologist who, in the past, has pushed speaking as the "best" way to communicate? I absolutely have. I share this example not only because it is an important first-person experience that needs to be shared but also because ableism exists across humans (including the author of this book), systems, structures, institutions, and professions. My profession is not exempt. As I have listened to the voices of those who communicate in ways in addition to, or other than, mouth speaking, I have learned that considering AAC only as a "last resort" is harmful and can be limiting. A few examples of AAC include speech generating communication devices, communication books, and picture exchange.

People being praised or accepted for appearing more "normal," whether because of speaking or because of some other skill or factor, can lead to what many in the neurodivergent community call "masking," which essentially is akin to erasure. The person has internalized that the ways that they exist are ostracized and then changes their behavior to match a predetermined norm that they have observed or been encouraged to emulate.

A prominent social influencer, Lyric Rivera, is autistic with ADHD and known online as Neurodivergent Rebel. Lyric describes masking in the following terms:

> Masking is when a neurodivergent Person either consciously or subconsciously hides, camouflages or masks their divergent traits in order to blend in or appear neuroTypical. . . . It's important to understand that this camouflaging, this blending in, this masking is something that many of us do in self-defense. It can be a subconscious thing. Some of us are not even aware we are doing it. It's something we do for safety and self-perseveration.

As a person who discovered my neurodivergence in my forties, I have spent a great deal of time trying to tease apart what parts of me are me and what parts are the mask I have worn to conceal the parts of me that did not earn favor. I do not have a visible disability, and therefore erasure of certain aspects of myself is optional for me, which is not the case for people with visible disabilities.

In Emily Page Ballou, Sharon daVanport, and Morénike Giwa Onaiwu's anthology *Sincerely, Your Autistic Child*, Lei Wiley-Mydske shares the following in her chapter titled "Change the World, Not Your Child":

> Redefine normal. Recognize that normal is subjective. Stimming, flapping, perseverance, and accommodating sensory preferences are not reasons to apologize. Your job is to build your child up, not tear them down due to a stranger's disapproving glare. Never apologize for your child being openly Autistic.

Society dictates which ways of existing are acceptable and which ones aren't. The way we look, move, communicate, eat, play, emote, speak, contribute, present, socialize, and attend all have acceptable and unacceptable versions. The Erasure of Disability happens because many of the ways that disabled people exist have been determined to be unacceptable. As a result, the choice for the disabled person is to either change oneself to present in the ways that are accepted or be subjected to ableism. Society's tendency to reward people who change themselves, or hide certain aspects of themselves, is driven by Erasure of Disability.

On an episode of *That Voice Podcast* with Sally Prosser that aired on April 18, 2021, Sally interviewed Mark Winski, a stuttering advocate and person who stutters. Mark promotes the message that stuttering is not something that needs to be hidden. Sally asked Mark what advice he would give to people who stutter, who think that they could never talk on a podcast. Mark responded by saying:

> You can. You can and you might stutter. And that's OK. Or you might not stutter. And that's OK, too. It's all OK. I think as soon as we stop, especially as a society that has these preconceived notions of what perfection is. It's very toxic at times. It's not just speech but also how we look, how we feel.

He goes on to talk about the importance of being able to show up as we are, from moment to moment, and how the energy we spend on making ourselves seem "perfect" robs us of joyful experiences.

What Does This Look Like in Action? Manifestations of Erasure of Disability

1. Praising someone for appearing "less disabled"

"I can barely tell you're blind!" or "You hardly stuttered at all today!" are examples of this manifestation. Statements like these are meant to be positive, but the underlying implication is "You have contained your disability to levels barely detectable by me. Good job!"

Though I have thankfully never found myself praising Dan for appearing less blind, I have had to check my interactions with Pete in relation to his dyslexia and spelling. He is working hard on reading and spelling to improve his literacy. When I praise him for his spelling, I make sure to point out to him that I am praising the hard work he has been putting into learning spelling and not the act of being a good speller. Pete defining his worth based on his ability to do something that his disability makes harder for him is a dangerous precedent and sends the message that when his disability is undetectable is when he is worthy of praise.

Challenge Yourself

When offering a compliment to a disabled person, make sure the compliment isn't inadvertently at the expense of the disability. It is best to avoid the assumption that the person desires to appear less disabled. If you know someone has set a personal goal to achieve a skill that is complicated by their disability and they are celebrating personal progress, celebration and praise are definitely appropriate. Just make sure that what you are praising is the same thing that the disabled person is celebrating. It's the difference between "Congratulations on your hard work!" and "It's a miracle!"

2. Accepting that "less disabled" or "no longer disabled" is always miraculous

Anytime the climax of a shared story about a disabled person is the moment the person does something counter to his disability, erasure is at work. We must remember that ableism is often under the surface of these stories, and they are usually accepted as miraculous without any information specific to the person in the story. To celebrate with someone when you have a personal relationship is appropriate. A bunch of strangers rejoicing in response to a viral video that gives us no more information than "was disabled, now isn't" is Erasure of Disability.

Challenge Yourself

I encourage you to think critically when whatever may be in front of you is suggesting that you should celebrate disability's disappearance. I am suggesting not that you apply blanket conclusions but rather that you apply what you have read in this book as you determine how you feel and whether ableism is at work. For example, when it comes to *The Secret Garden,* Pete and I have discussed how Colin's isolation and general state of unhappiness was a sad part of his story and that there is great triumph in his rehabilitation, because of what it means for his mental and physical health. Colin being able to walk through the garden isn't the pinnacle of the story. Colin finally finding happiness and excitement about his future is the pinnacle of the story. Being able to walk is not a prerequisite for happiness or a bright future. Breaking down individual situations can help you identify what parts are ableist and why.

3. Stigmatizing support and noninclusive definitions of independence

The common preoccupation with independence reinforces stigma that contributes to Erasure of Disability. A person being able to "do it all" without help is boasted as the gold standard in many modern societies, and this ideal is an insidious form of ableism. If not needing any support from anyone means I am superior, what does that say about people who do need support?

The definition of *independence* is simply to be independent, but a synonym of *independence* is self-government. Interestingly, the definition of *autonomy* is the right or condition of self-government. Remember that being independent does not imply that you are doing everything on your own but, rather, that you are making the decisions to govern your own life. That can happen with, or without, support.

Challenge Yourself

Reframe the way you view and talk about independence. Do you consider a CEO who delegates responsibilities lacking in competence because she does not single-handedly meet every need? If you cook dinner one night but instead order pizza the next night because you're busy, does this mean your independence was compromised the second night? Or does it mean your circumstances varied from one day to the next and you maintained your independence by getting dinner on the table in a different way?

If this version of independence makes sense to you, apply it to your kids. If you constantly frame *independent* to mean "without help or support," not only will your kids potentially feel shame for accepting support when they think they are supposed to be able to do everything on their own, but they also will innately hold misconceptions about others who utilize help and support.

You can support autonomy and independence in ways that don't fuel stigma related to support. Instead of "You tied your shoes all by yourself! You didn't need anyone to help you!" try something like "You had everything you needed today to get your shoes tied without me!" This type of reframing conveys that a child who ties his shoes without support one day and asks for help the next day is independent both days, because he did what he needed to get the desired result. The next day might look like "Today, you were feeling rushed and knew you would need my assistance to get your shoes tied in time. I'm glad you were able to take care of that need."

4. Productivity as a status symbol

The practice of establishing personal worth through what, and how much, a person produces is another way that Erasure of Disability manifests. When a person's brain and/or body have needs that don't align with the standards our employment systems have established, it leads to employment inequity and/or disabled people pushing their brains and bodies beyond their limits to try to keep up.

Challenge Yourself

We can make space for people who produce differently than we do and recognize that their contributions can look different and still be useful. We can go a step further and recognize that a person's ability to produce is not what dictates their worth or value.

A simple strategy I like to implement with my kids that helps me keep my thoughts about worth and productivity in check is telling my kids that their best is enough and then leaving room for their best to look different from day to day. We frequently have conversations in our house about how we are feeling, and when my kids have low energy or are feeling sad about something, I acknowledge those feelings and allow for reductions in expectations, providing help when I might not typically help, postponing tasks, or simply allowing them to go unfinished. We talk about the importance of listening to your body and honoring what it needs, as well as the importance of rest.

Bring It Home

If you talk about triumphs that negate disability—for example, a wheelchair user taking a few steps—in front of your kids, make sure to add important nuance for your kids to consider. You might mention that for every wheelchair user who has an acquired disability that can be rehabilitated, there is at least one physically disabled person who will not rehabilitate and will continue to use a wheelchair. Pointing out that triumphs are individual, rather than implying that walking is always better than using a wheelchair, is important to these conversations.

Aaron Slater, Illustrator by Andrea Beaty is a beautiful children's story about a dyslexic child who thinks that trying harder will help him keep up. He struggles with reading and writing in first grade but decides that second grade will be his year, if he just works hard enough. Aaron is given a writing assignment.

> And so Aaron does what young Aaron must do.
> He works on his story like the rest of Grade Two.
> He writes through the evening.
> He writes through the night.
> He writes and he writes
> till the dawn's early light.
>
> Then he drags off to school with his shoes filled with lead
> and his stomach in knots and a pain in his head.

Aaron is a gifted artist and often finds himself drawing instead of writing. On the day his writing assignment is due, he stands in front of his class and looks at his paper, which includes only a drawing of a flower. He closes his eyes and starts to share a story about a magical flower, from his imagination. The illustrations in the book reveal the beauty of the story he is telling, as it exists in his mind, which reveals his strengths to be the hero of the story. Eventually, he finishes.

> And when the quest ends and the sweet flower dies,
> the students all gasp and Miss Lila Greer cries.
> The silence that follows rattles his heart.
> He tries to say something, but where could he start?

He turns in a paper with no words at all,
then blinks back a tear and escapes to the hall
where Miss Lila finds him by the slate-colored wall.

Aaron is expecting to be scolded because his story was not in writing but instead is thanked by his teacher. Ultimately, Aaron recognizes that what he has to offer is beautiful and valuable and that revealing a part of himself that makes him stand out helped him get to a healthier place. Books like these can be priceless for kids with similar struggles, as sometimes they feel as if aspects of their journey go unseen.

However, they also can be impactful for kids who cannot relate to the experience. Giving your kids the chance to empathize with situations that don't affect them directly will make them better friends, family members, and neighbors.

13

"CAN I PET YOUR DOG?"

DISRESPECT OF DISABILITY SUPPORTS

There is a long white "stick," as you may see it, but we call it a cane. It might sound crazy to describe it this way, but it is our eyes. We use this mobility tool to feel our surroundings. Whether objects in our path, or discovering curbs and staircases, it helps us travel with ease of use. Never jump, grab, or hold the other end of the cane to tease, or offer help. One time, I was walking and someone offered to help and proceeds to pick up the other end of my cane as I'm holding the side I needed to hold on to. I was disgusted—couldn't believe that this person even remotely thought it was a smart idea to do such a thing, completely making me look like I'm an immobilized, human-sized animal and I'm getting guided by a harness of some sort.

THIS EXCERPT IS from an April 2014 article for *Thought Catalog* by Daniel Romero called "5 Things You Should Never Do to a Blind

Person." When you are used to the feedback that a mobility aid gives you, and you rely on that feedback for safety, having a stranger take that feedback away from you is extremely disorienting. If you use your eyes to take in information while walking on the street, imagine a stranger rushing up to you, putting a blindfold on you, and pulling you around. How safe would you feel?

In a video called "Oops, You Did an Ableism," deaf and disabled activist Jessica Kellgren-Fozard talks about what it feels like to have her equipment disrespected.

> When you insult someone's medical equipment, it feels like you're insulting a part of them. I rely on things like my mobility aids and I don't have another option. Your belittling it doesn't make me feel better about that.

The aids, equipment, and accommodations that disabled people utilize are vitally important and can ensure safety, health, independence, and more. Unfortunately, disabled people often report that many others are unfamiliar with how equipment and aids should, and should not, be interacted with. This results in frequent interactions that include the Disrespect of Disability Supports. Many disabled people consider their aids and equipment to be extensions of their body, and unauthorized touch of their equipment is like unauthorized touch of their body.

Activist and content creator Gem Hubbard, who goes by wheelsonheels online, discusses Disrespect of Disability Supports in her video "10 Reasons Why You Should Never Touch a Wheelchair (Without Asking)." Followers of hers who use wheelchairs and mobility aids shared how it makes them feel when someone disrespects their equipment, and Gem used their input in the video.

> OK, so the comment that came up the most was, it's rude. You wouldn't touch another nondisabled person. You

wouldn't pick up a nondisabled person and move them out of the way. If someone's bag was in the way, you would probably ask them, the owner of that bag, to move it, so why should it be any different for someone's mobility aid? It is rude and it's disrespectful.

Gem explains logistical considerations that non–wheelchair users wouldn't be aware of, such as her hands getting pinched and crushed when people decide to push her wheelchair without her consent or knowledge. She mentions additional important factors, including how expensive mobility aids are, the need to sanitize the equipment after it is touched, and the emotional impact that these encounters have.

It isn't just equipment and aids that are subject to disrespect. Accommodations are often treated as last resorts for people who "aren't trying hard enough" and, therefore, subject to scrutiny and stigma. On the podcast *ADHD for Smart Ass Women*, host Tracy Otsuka interviewed Amanda Smith in November 2022. Amanda has multiple sclerosis, which caused lesions on her brain that resulted in symptoms that are the same as the symptoms of ADHD. She explains how her life changed after the onset of her acquired ADHD and how accommodations that she had never before used became so important to her.

> I did know what works for me but it didn't necessarily work that way anymore. Because I wasn't born ADHD, things were just easy. I didn't have to think about doing . . . the things. They just happened. And so, now, I would look at my schedule and am thinking "OK, I have a kid that needs to go to a doctor's appointment. I need to schedule a doctor's appointment. I need to work. How do all these things fit together? Am I double booking myself?" I had never had to use a planner before. I just remembered things. So now, it actually became an effort.

Amanda goes on to talk about the ways that her challenges with memory affected her work as an IRS auditor.

> In Alabama, I was the superstar. I was the next one in management. I was the next one that . . . I knew the things. Everyone would come and ask me questions. And I move up here and I felt like such a fraud. Because I'm thinking, "I have no clue where all of this went to." It was just like waking up one morning and going "Huh. Who is that chick?" Because she left the building. She's not there. I look like her. I maybe even sound like her. But she's gone. . . . I look at it now and think, Holy crap. This life would have been much easier if I would have learned all these tips and tricks and hacks and things when I was younger. But you don't expect to wake up one morning and feel like a completely different person.

Amanda not being able to do the things she used to do without support made her feel like a different person, even though she was the same person. The necessity of accommodations can affect people's self-worth because of the stigma that they carry. Accommodations can be so stigmatized, in fact, that accommodation stigma has its own nicknames and alternatives. *Special treatment stigma* is a term applied to accommodations in education, and there is a push to call work accommodations *job aids* instead.

Medication is another example of something that is helpful to disabled people but is stigmatized. In *The Center Cannot Hold*, Elyn Saks shares her journey with mental illness and how medication stigma affected her.

> In addition, I wasn't in any sort of treatment or therapy, or taking any kind of medication. There were plenty of

indications that I should do something—talk to somebody, take some kind of pill. I knew that much; I was not, after all, stupid. But pills were bad, drugs were bad. Crutches were bad. If you needed a crutch, that meant you were a cripple. It means that you were not strong enough to manage on your own. It meant you were weak, and worthless.

Later in the book, she circles back to the same struggle, which had become very familiar over the years. The hesitation to take medication became a common and recurring theme, as she made attempts to discontinue medication that were followed by dangerous and scary episodes of psychosis. She registered situations as failures. She explains:

> For so many years, I'd restricted the "crutch" of the meds— to use them meant I was weak of will, weak of character. But now I began to question my own absoluteness. For instance, if I'd had a broken leg and a crutch was required, I'd have used it without ever thinking twice. Was my brain not worth tending to at least as much as my leg? The fact was, I had a condition that required medicine. If I didn't use it, I got sick; if I used it, I got better. I don't know why I had to keep learning that the hard way, but I did.

Let me clearly state that I understand there are many reasons why people view medication with skepticism. Those concerns could be related to side effects, interactions with other medications, cultural considerations, and so on. Critical evaluation and stigma are two different things, though. A person has every right to decide if medication is right for them, and stigma shouldn't be one of the reasons why people might choose to avoid medication.

The importance of aids, equipment, and accommodations should not be understated and often extends beyond the intended users.

Allison Murray-Nikkel explains how captions on video content can be helpful for an audience wider than those in the d/Deaf community and people who have hearing loss in an article for Empire Caption Solutions called "Closed Captions and Neurodivergence." In the article, specific diagnoses and conditions are listed, with an explanation of how closed captions can be helpful. For example, sensory processing disorder (SPD) is listed with the following information:

> SPD is another condition that often overlaps with Autism/ASD. Some people with sensory integration challenges may find it difficult to process both visual and auditory information at the same time. Using captions allows someone with SPD to take everything in through a visual format and can make it easier for them to process and comprehend. For some individuals, certain sounds and tones may be especially unpleasant or even painful, so they need to be able to access that information visually instead.

In *What's That Pig Outdoors? A Memoir of Deafness*, Henry Kisor talks about the first kinds of adaptive equipment that he used, and what they meant to him.

> Two decades ago Sam's box and the Sensicall seemed to be merely conveniences, like refrigerators and washing machines. They were marvelous gadgets, and I thought I'd miss them if they weren't around but I could live without them, as I had all my life. Of course, I missed the point. Modern conveniences are instruments of freedom. A life without something to cool perishables and freshen clothing would be a very different one. We would need to devote a great deal of time and energy to basic survival tasks such as obtaining fresh food and clean clothes. Life without fridges

and washers would be tolerable, but our spheres of activity would be severely limited. We would have less freedom to do things that matter—such as communicating with the rest of the world.

Now it seems that, crude as those two early devices were, they meant the beginning of the end of my isolation—isolation from other people. Those who hear cannot imagine how grindingly lonely deafness often can be. A comfortable home can feel like a maximum-security prison if there is no easy means of communicating with the outside.

In *Year of the Tiger*, Alice Wong talks about the empowerment she experienced when transitioning into her first electric wheelchair.

It quickly became apparent that I did not have enough upper-body strength to push myself, and I soon transitioned into my first electric wheelchair. The clouds parted, the disabled angels sang, and I took my rightful place on my motorized throne. It was total liberation: I was in a comfortable position and, most important, in control. I didn't need my parents or other people to move me around—a push of the joystick and I zipped around at dangerously fast speeds. I could express myself through movement for the first time. It may seem ghastly to most nondisabled people to rejoice in the usage of a wheelchair, but I consider it part of my natural development as an autonomous human being.

In *Have Dog, Will Travel*, Stephen Kuusisto writes about the day that he and other guide dog students set off for New York City.

In my junior year of college I'd wanted desperately to travel to Manhattan to hear a renowned poet read his work at

92nd Street Y. But I had no one to accompany me. I stayed
home in Geneva and listened to Billie Holiday records and
in the manner of young people, felt my deprivation bitterly.
I could have taken the Greyhound bus, but what then? How
would I walk alone? How would I manage the subway? The
world had been beyond my reach. Now going to New York
with a dog, a powerful dog, seemed like something out of
a superhero comic. As our train moved beside the Hudson
River I stroked Corey's silky ears and then, softly, I began
to cry. I'd spent my adult life living as a pallid child. And
fearful. But with my dog, the mill wheel of progress was
turning inside me. I was poised to walk New York City, to
learn it—to learn I could do it. A woman across the aisle
asked if I was okay. I told her I was fine, that I was about
to be free.

What Does This Look Like in Action? Manifestations of Disrespect of Disability Supports

1. Touching or interacting with a person's equipment or aids without permission

Petting a person's service dog, touching a person's wheelchair, and
grabbing someone's cane are all examples of this manifestation. Even
though most guide dogs are clearly marked with vests that say some
version of DON'T PET ME, many guide and support dog handlers
report strangers violating this rule. In a video on AMI: Accessible
Media Inc.'s YouTube channel called "AM I Right? Don't Pet My
Guide Dog," Beth Deer talks about why it is important to respect
service dog handlers by refraining from distracting their service dog.
Beth explains:

Listen, I love dogs. Dogs are cute. Dogs are amazing. Dogs are life. There comes a point when people have to understand when that dog is working, he's a hearing aid, a white cane, a wheelchair, even a prosthetic limb. He's a mobility aid, a tool to enhance someone's life who has a disability. . . . Please do not distract a service dog. They are constantly having to think about what they have to do. So when you distract them, it breaks that train of thought and they could potentially be putting their owner in danger.

Challenge Yourself

This one is very easy and straightforward. First of all, refrain from petting or distracting service dogs. If the handler and service dog seem to be in a moment of rest, Beth Deer says that it is OK to ask about petting the dog, but be mindful of when you do this. Knowing that disabled people report a constant barrage of attention that they often do not wish for, the better decision might be to just let the dog and handler do their thing. Educating your children about service dogs is also important, as you never know where they might encounter a service dog and handler. If they are educated, they can be a model to their peers of what is appropriate. The YouTube video that was quoted earlier in this chapter is educational and easy for children to understand.

Second, don't touch someone's mobility, adaptive, or assistive equipment unless you have been asked to do so. The list of assistive devices is long. Instead of determining if you should touch something without asking based on whether it is considered adaptive equipment, instead use ownership to determine your right to touch it without asking. Does it belong to you? If yes, then feel free to do what you wish. If no, then you should always ask permission, and wait for an answer, before touching or interacting with any equipment.

When it comes to educating your kids, this aligns with discussions of consent. If you teach your children to respect the boundaries of others and always ask for consent before acting upon someone else, it will not be difficult for them to make the leap to extending that to equipment. In our house, we talk a lot about ownership and consent, which applies to bodies, clothing, toys, and beyond. This is foundational to autonomy and sense of self and is beneficial to people on both sides of an interaction, and not only when it comes to disability equipment. If your child has a peer who uses a wheelchair, teach your child to always ask before pushing the peer in the wheelchair, regardless of whether the peer controls or propels the wheelchair.

I have been very deliberate in making sure that Dan's adaptive equipment is never treated like toys. Even though many children are curious about his cane, I have never allowed other kids, even Pete, to play with it. Ultimately, it is up to Dan to determine who can do what with his cane, but when he was much younger and it was my responsibility to protect his cane, I modeled an expectation of respect for it as an important tool. If your child is curious about another child's cane, make sure to teach your child not to grab or take it. When we play at playgrounds, Dan often leaves his cane somewhere before climbing onto elevated play structures. I try to keep an eye on it, knowing that it will be something that other kids are curious about. I don't get upset when children, especially very small children, grab the cane when it is unattended. Its novelty makes it naturally interesting.

What is most helpful to me is when other parents step in and explain to their kids that the cane belongs to someone else and that they are not allowed to play with it. I will take that on, when I need to, but it is refreshing when I don't have to. I also dream of the day when education has reached enough parents and children that we can simply leave the cane wherever Dan feels is best and trust that it will be there when he returns.

2. Discounting or disregarding the importance of disability aids and accommodations

Often, people use the information they have about another person to decide that person doesn't actually need the supports they claim to benefit from. Examples of this include people who can read using audiobooks and people who can hear using closed captioning. There are numerous reasons why alternative access works for people, but unfortunately, a lack of understanding often leads to rigidity regarding who gets to use what. Though some people may technically have the skill to do something a certain way, other factors affect their ability to access that skill consistently enough, or for a long enough duration, for it to be the most efficient way of doing the thing.

Over the last few years, as I have discovered my ADHD and gotten closer to unpacking my own ableism, this manifestation has played out personally. I have long had a complicated relationship with reading. Reading itself has never been challenging for me, but reading whole books has. The only period of my life when I finished a lot of books was in fourth grade. I imagine it was at about this age that my ability to read was somewhat novel to me, which is very reinforcing to my ADHD. In fourth grade, my classmates and I also received lots of praise for reading. I remember paper ice cream cones taped on the wall and getting to add a paper "scoop" to our cone for every book that we read. I am a recovering perfectionistic people pleaser, and the ice cream cone challenge must have been a big deal to me because my memory has held onto it. My ice cream cone stretched all the way up the wall and halfway across the ceiling.

After fourth grade, I recall finishing only a few books, and they were so enthralling that they engaged all my attention. I remember often falling asleep while reading, and I also became really good at grazing text to find the key points instead of reading pages in their entirety. This is how I made it through high school, college, and graduate school. After finishing formal education, I started collecting books that looked very interesting to me, but most of them ended up with a bookmark somewhere between the first and third chapters. My inability to finish these books always felt like failure to me. I assumed the worst about myself—that I must be really lazy, that I wasn't the "intellectual" I had hoped to be, that I lacked whatever it was that made people readers.

When I was in my midthirties, I discovered audiobooks. At the time, my job had me doing home visits, which meant that I spent a lot of time in my car. I started devouring audiobooks and was exhilarated. When talking about the books, though, I always felt I needed to make the distinction that I listened to them rather than *read* them. Technically, it is accurate, but my fixation on the difference revealed my shame and, it turns out, was my internalized ableism demanding attention.

Fast-forward to 2020, when I was doing research about reading to try to better support Pete after his diagnoses of dyslexia and ADHD. As I learned more about these diagnoses and their impact on reading, I started to make connections to my own history with reading. I started to figure out that when my body is expected to be still and all my attention is supposed to focus on the words I am reading, my brain goes in too many different directions to comprehend and store the words I am reading. My eyes read the words, but my brain is often attending to other thoughts, so I don't process them. When listening to a book, though, and keeping my body busy with a task that I don't need to think about, the part of my brain that needs to be available for listening and comprehension is freed up.

Learning from disabled people has helped me understand that the best form of access is the one that is the most helpful. There are some who don't count audiobooks as reading, but I now understand that an audiobook allows you to experience the story just the same as reading words from a page does. I could deny myself the form of access that is best for me, for the sake of fitting into a box that society has built, but then I would miss out on so many books.

It is not uncommon for people's benefit from alternative access to be disregarded, minimized, and/or shamed. Even though these access methods can often be easily obtained and do not negatively affect others, they are still sometimes discouraged.

Challenge Yourself

Think about the tools you use in your everyday life. Do you set an alarm to wake you in the morning? Do you use a day planner or calendar app on your phone or other device? These are aids that people utilize to support them in managing executive function, which is the mental processes we use to plan, organize, focus, pay attention, and track time (among many other things).

Do you ever turn music on, or off, when you need to focus? Have you ever asked a teacher, professor, or boss for an extension on an assignment or project deadline? These are accommodations. I would wager that everyone uses aids and accommodations to manage the demands of daily life. As technology advances, we find ourselves with more tools that are designed to support us in what we want and need to accomplish each day. What does and doesn't help or work varies from person to person. Don't make assumptions about why something does or does not work for another person and steer yourself away from the idea that there is a finite amount of support that a person should need. If we can reach a point where we don't make up silly rules about who can and cannot access the world in specific ways, and what accommodations we will and won't allow people to utilize, we create freedom and improved access for everyone.

When it comes to kids, we can honor this by being open to allowing variance in how they exist in the world. A personal example that comes to mind as a parent is tying shoes. Many children might struggle with tying their shoes, for a variety of reasons, and in parenting groups I see the issue come up frequently. There are different methods and countless online videos with demonstrations of how to teach your kid to tie their shoes. Shoe tying seems to be a skill that many parents value, even though there are numerous no-tie options now available.

Encouraging your kids to learn new skills is important, but what happens next is where we can be mindful of our reactions and decisions about how to proceed. Some kids struggle to learn, and if your child is struggling, it can be easy to jump to the conclusion that they aren't trying hard enough. Is it that they aren't trying hard enough, or is something about this making it more challenging? Figuring out what barriers might be causing struggle is an important step, as is deciding if shoe tying is a battle worth picking. This will vary from parent to parent, and I'm not suggesting that it is or isn't.

What I can tell you about Pete is that he does know how to tie his shoes. It is a battle we picked, and we persisted until he learned. What happened next is why I am telling this story. He knows how to tie his shoes, so we bought tie-shoes. He never chose to wear them. His ADHD makes it unlikely that he will choose a task like tying his shoes unless he really loves the shoes and is motivated enough to wear them, which he only chooses to do occasionally. His brain is wired to bypass tasks that do not grab or hold his attention or that he is not motivated to take on.

Does this mean he can't do any tasks that take more than a moment? Not at all. He has willingly taken on tasks that take quite some time to complete, like sorting boxes of LEGOS and cataloging comic books. Often, it is not a conscious decision to pass on something, like tie-shoes, but rather more about his thoughts being on something else and him subconsciously taking care of getting his shoes on while attending to other thoughts. Occasionally, he finds a pair of shoes that he absolutely loves that require tying and, in those cases, we ask if he would rather take the time to tie them or swap out the tie laces with no-tie laces. Accepting that he is unlikely to choose to tie his shoes helps us avoid unnecessary power struggles about shoes, and buying him shoes that he can slip on means that we don't waste money. We could stand firm in the fact that he *can* tie his shoes and therefore must, but we have chosen a different way. This accommodation supports peace in our home, as do the many aids and accommodations that we utilize.

3. Nondisabled people using disability-designated spaces

People deciding to use spaces that have been adapted to be accessible, when they do not need to, is another example of Disrespect of Disability Supports. Everyone reading this is familiar with what an accessible parking space is and probably already knows that it is considered inconsiderate to park in one if you do not need to. Regardless of this common understanding, people who need accessible parking spaces still commonly report not having access to them because of people without disabilities parking there, or parking in the marked-off area next to them. This can also apply to accessible stalls in bathrooms. When numerous stalls are open, people sometimes choose the accessible stall, which leaves it unnecessarily occupied when a wheelchair or mobility aid user needs it. The accessible stall is also sometimes needed when the changing tables in a restroom aren't sufficient for individuals with complex toileting needs.

In a video called "What to Do When Someone Parks in the Access Aisle: Episode 1," found on the Facebook page for disabled comedian, actor, and writer Zach Anner, humor is used to educate about accessible parking. Zach partnered with Jordan from BraunAbility, which is a mobility company, to make the video. Jordan explains that the area marked with lines on either side of an accessible parking spot is called the access aisle and that 42 percent of people surveyed don't know what it is for. He goes on to share that the access aisle creates the space required for the use of a wheelchair ramp. During the video, a car parks in the access aisle and Zach asks what they are going to do. The BraunAbility representative reports that 74 percent of people surveyed said that, in the case of a blocked access aisle, they would just climb in through a door or window. Zach then demonstrates why that solution is problematic and unrealistic. Zach, who has cerebral palsy, comedically and unsuccessfully attempts to pull himself through the car's driver-side window. He and Jordan conclude the video with a simpler solution, which is "Don't park in the access aisle."

Challenge Yourself

In every parking lot, there are far more non-accessible parking spots than accessible ones, so if you do not have an accessible parking tag, park in one of those. Don't park in accessible spaces, or in the access spaces around them. I understand the temptation to park there— maybe you're in a rush and think you'll only be a moment—but think about how frustrated you would feel if someone blocked access to your vehicle and you had to wait there for them to come out, or go inside to try to find them. Don't use the accessible bathroom stall unless all other stalls are full and there isn't anyone with mobility needs in line.

In addition, don't make judgments about people you see utilizing accessible parking. We have already learned about invisible disability and understand that we don't have, and are not entitled to, the reasons why a person needs accessible parking. Take a deep breath and remember that your frustration about parking isn't actually about people who use accessible parking but is likely related to your personal time constraints or feelings about the availability of spaces you can park in. Consider this: Do you find yourself frustrated about accessible parking when there is a spot open right next to one that you can park in? Or does your frustration only surface when there aren't any open spots close to the entrance? Human nature causes us to want to blame someone, but disabled people aren't the ones we are actually mad at.

4. The "disability tax" and inequities in disability supports and aides

The "disability tax" is a term used by the disability community to refer to how much more money a disabled person pays just to live than a nondisabled person. On *Where's Your Dog?*, blogger Meagan writes

> The free market was supposed to help us all. The invisible hand of competition was supposed to keep prices reasonable. We were supposed to have choice. Unfortunately, capitalism can't accommodate markets that are too small to inspire competition, nor can it liberate us from monopolies that keep prices extortionately high.

James Moore gives an example of this in an article in the *Independent* called "The True Cost of Being Disabled Goes Far Beyond Just the Physical." He tells how being offered gloves is a common occurrence when purchasing a wheelchair, and how gloves that are marked as "assistive" are more expensive, even if they are the same gloves that are marketed another way. He tells of how a wheelchair basketball teammate spent about twenty-five dollars for gel-filled gloves that were marked as being for wheelchair users, and therefore better, that only held up for few days.

> Remove the term "wheelchair" or "disabled" from the product and instead add "cycling" and you'll get a perfectly serviceable pair from Sports Direct for under fiver. Aldi has sold a gel filled pair for £3 in one of its sporadic cycling sales.

A markup from approximately five to twenty-five dollars is one example of the disability tax. I did a quick search for magnifier devices and used the words "for the visually impaired" for one search and "for rock collectors" for the other. The magnifiers for the visually impaired search took me to a website that sells adaptive and assistive equipment, and the magnifiers were sixty-five to seventy dollars. For rock collectors, I found a magnifier for less than twenty. Is it possible that the more expensive magnifiers are slightly better? Certainly. But are they forty dollars better?

The disability tax shows up in a number of ways, including:

- Energy costs related to equipment that uses electricity
- Food costs related to dietary needs and food delivery
- Wages for support workers
- Transportation costs related to the scheduling parameters and reliability of free public transit or fatigue that prohibits short trips on foot
- Medication costs
- The costs of assistive technology, like accessibility software

It isn't uncommon to see online fundraisers for people needing electronic wheelchairs or ramps in their homes.

Most of these examples relate to people with physical disabilities. Neurodivergent people utilize aides and supports as well, and are not exempt from the disability tax. I have noticed, though, that some of the executive function aids and supports are gradually being added in as standard features in operating systems of popular devices. Scheduling features, as well as task- and time-tracking features, are becoming readily available without needing to pay an extra fee. I suspect that this is because as more and more people started to see how they made their lives easier, developers started noticing and started incorporating these features to make their products more appealing to the consumer. Companies considered the costs related to software additions and changes worth it.

Challenge Yourself

Most of us don't feel as if we have much power over the ways that companies market and price their products. More people being aware of the disability tax, however, can make a difference if we, the consumers, call it out when we see it.

Another way that we can push back on disability tax is through opening ourselves up to adaptive equipment. Adaptive equipment and supportive aids can be helpful to people who don't have diagnoses. When more people use an item, it influences the market in a favorable way, which typically drives the cost down. Not too many years ago, you could only get fidget spinners through websites that sold products to support neurodivergent children. In recent years, it has been discovered that fidgets are appealing and helpful to many people, and now fidgets are more readily available and much less expensive than they were a few years ago.

If you or someone you care about has a task that is harder for them, or they could use some support with, do an online search for adaptive tools for that task. When I have to do a lot of writing by hand, I often borrow one of Pete's pencil grips, because I can write a lot more before hand fatigue sets in. A diagnosed disability is rarely required to obtain and benefit from adaptive products. An elderly relative, for example, might benefit from adaptive silverware—and the more people who purchase adaptive silverware, the more accessible and affordable adaptive silverware becomes.

There is an additional benefit to opening ourselves up to the use of adaptive aids and equipment. Wider use decreases the stigma attached to said items. In an article on the website Thinking Person's Guide to Autism, "What the Fidget Spinners Fad Reveals about Disability

Discrimination," Aiyana Bailin talks about how fidget spinners, and disabled people's need to fidget, used to be terribly stigmatized. That changed when a teenaged entrepreneur with ADHD turned fidget spinners into a fad, and turned quite a profit doing it. Fidget spinners' popularity was not necessarily an embrace of disability-supportive aids, unfortunately, but more of a capitalist venture that led to fidget spinners being destigmatized. Bailin writes,

> This is important. Really important, so read this next sentence twice: **Something that was considered entirely pathological and in dire need of correction when done by disabled people is now perfectly acceptable because it is being done by non-disabled people.** This should make you stop and think, especially if you are someone who works with, educates, or researches people with diagnoses like autism.

By opening ourselves up to the idea of using potentially stigmatized adaptive equipment, we can move away from destimatizing through fads, and move closer to destigmatizing through acceptance of people as individuals meeting their individual needs, with the use of adaptive equipment and aids, and not because it is trendy or profitable.

5. Medication stigma

Though medication isn't technically equipment, it is essential for many, and disabled people often face stigma related to the medications they need. Medication stigma seems most common when medication is being used to treat the brain, like for those with mental health conditions and ADHD. These medications improve a person's quality of life and should be respected the same as medications people take to help with pain, organ function, and illness.

Challenge Yourself

You are entitled to opinions about medication, but your personal experiences and opinions are your own. If someone tells you that they take medication, please resist the urge to tell them about a supplement, oil, or other solution, unless you have a close relationship. Remember that someone else making the choice to take medication affects your life zero percent. You don't have to believe the medication would be right for you to accept that it is right for others.

Most of us have explained medicine to our kids and have helped them understand that medications are something that can help us. If you find yourself in the position to talk to your kids about types of medications that you or they have never taken, you can include notes about how everyone's body is different and the medicine different people need varies. Try to avoid adding things like "You are lucky because you don't need to take a medicine like x does," as this reinforces stigma by suggesting that a person who needs a certain kind of medication is at a disadvantage and worthy of pity. Is it true that certain kinds of medication come with downsides? Of course. In situations where you don't know how a person feels about the medications they take, though, it isn't your place to assign tragedy to someone else's supports. You come close to disrespecting someone's private information when you have to go into detail to explain why you are suggesting something is problematic.

Like many other examples we have come across, this is an instance of applying assumption across the board and casting a dark shadow unnecessarily. "That person takes that medicine because it helps them" is safe and respectful. Sticking closer to the facts and what you actually know, and resisting the urge to pass judgment or assign feelings, will keep you farther from ableism.

Bring It Home

Providing your children explicit education on disability aids and equipment will help equip them to avoid this form of ableism. The following excerpt is from the book *Guide Dogs! A Kids Book About Guide & Assistance Dogs* by Lionel Paxton.

> You shouldn't pet a Guide Dog without asking—doing this is like taking the steering wheel away from someone driving a car. This is very dangerous as it puts you, the dog and the blind person at risk because the dog is distracted. The owner may not allow you, not because they don't like you, but because the Guide Dog only gets praise as a reward for working and if someone else was giving them their reward they may not want to work.

Following disabled people on social media is another way to find educational opportunities for you and your kids to learn more. Anthony S. Ferraro is a Paralympic athlete and content creator who shares videos that always start with "I'm blind and this is how I . . ." He talks through how he uses his cane in certain activities and how access happens in a variety of situations as he adventures and lives his life.

Another way to empower your children to avoid this form of ableism is through celebrating how the ways we modify to accommodate for disability bring rich experiences and beauty to disabled people and others. The book *Moses Goes to a Concert* by Isaac Millman tells the story of Moses and his Deaf friends going to a concert.

> "She has no shoes!" Moses signs in surprise. The teacher smiles and signs, "She is deaf, too. She follows the orchestra by feeling the vibrations of the music through her stocking

feet." Then Mr. Samuels takes eleven balloons out of his black bag and hands one to each of his students. "Oh! What beautiful balloons!" Anna signs. "Hold them on your lap," signs Mr. Samuels. "They'll help you feel the music."

This book includes illustrations that show how to sign numerous words, phrases, and sentences in American Sign Language (ASL). According to the National Association of the Deaf (NAD), ASL is a visual language that incorporates hand shape, hand placement, hand movement, facial expressions, and body movements. ASL is used predominately in the United States and many parts of Canada.

I find that children are usually fascinated by braille, and I imagine the same is true for sign language and many other things unique to disability, like aids, equipment, and accommodations. There is great power in modeling not only respect but also interest and appreciation. Though sign language and braille aren't aids and equipment, they can be subject to disrespect just the same. Educating your children about them, alongside supports, while framing them as positive, is another way to steer children away from disrespect of the different ways disabled people access the world.

14

"IT WAS JUST A JOKE"

OTHERING DISABILITY

I N *SAY HELLO*, Carly Findlay tells a story about when she was a baby and her mom once asked a stranger outside of a store to look after Carly for a moment while she quickly ran inside. She returned to find a group of strangers peering into Carly's pram.

> That moment in the pram was the start of what life had in store for me. It can be relentless. I can't think of a day outside of the house when I haven't been stared at, intruded upon or abused because of my appearance. Some people look away—which can hurt as much as the stares. These reactions can change my mood. Most days I start off feeling happy, excited, anticipating a great time ahead, and feeling good about my skin and appearance. Even though the stares, comments and discrimination happen frequently, they're always unexpected. I like to think the next person I encounter will simply greet me with a smile, or I'll be able to get through the day, comment-free.

Othering Disability tells us the lie that disabled people are so unlike nondisabled people that we must categorize them as a separate group and treat them accordingly. The ways that disabled people have been othered have varied over time periods and cultures. An article for *Renaissance Universal* called "The History of Disability: A History of 'Otherness,'" by Jayne Clapton and Jennifer Fitzgerald, talks about disability and othering.

> Bodily difference has for centuries determined social structures by defining certain bodies as the norm, and defining those which fall outside the norm as "Other"; with the degree of "Otherness" being defined by the degree of variation from the norm. In doing this, we have created an artificial "paradigm of humanity" into which some of us fit neatly, and others fit very badly. Life outside the paradigm of humanity is likely to be characterized by isolation and abuse.
>
> The story we have recorded of the lives of people with disability is a story of life lived on the margins. For people with disability, their history is largely a history of silence. The lives of people with disability have not only been constructed as "Other," but frequently as "the Other" of "the Other." People with disability are marginalized even by those who are themselves marginalized.

Othering can show up in many forms. In addition to systemic othering, insidious forms are also common. In *Have Dog, Will Travel*, a group of guide dog students talk about being othered for their blindness by being treated as a spectacle: "You're in a restaurant and twelve other folks, strangers all, are eyeing you because you're significantly different. Sighted people enjoy novelty and you're the novelty du jour. Even if you're just chewing a muffin, you're entertainment." I have been taken aback on numerous occasions when people blatantly stare at Dan. They watch him as if he was a species of bird they have never seen before.

In *We've Got This*, Debra Keenahan tells of a time when her family's outing was ruined by othering.

> On a family outing to a parkland area, we encountered an example of careless parenting. When we got out of the car, another family in the car park found our dwarfism such a source of hilarity the adults tried to photograph us with their phones. They didn't even try to hide their actions. We quickly moved between and around cars to block their view from us. Fortunately, we were not followed. We'd planned to visit for the whole afternoon. But we left after only two hours—and a further three instances of unsolicited photographing.

On her Facebook page Nurshable, my friend Sarah shared a post in January 2023 about how othering shows up in disability awareness activities. Sarah explains how her son came home from school with a disability awareness bracelet and was a bit surprised when she mentioned that she is disabled. She goes on to talk about how she was paid to teach disability awareness when she was in school.

> I don't other myself the way disability awareness programs other people. Disability awareness programs were, and I suspect still are literally "look, these people exist. They are different. Here, button up your shirt with socks on your hands. Walk around this room with a blindfold on using this stick. Put these earplugs in, and imagine they make it so you don't hear anything at all."
>
> My presentation was more "y'all sound like you're whispering. It's kind of annoying. I lipread but people are

bad at remembering to look at people when they talk. Do I miss hearing? Uh. Do you miss flying? No. You never did it. What's to miss? I'm normal. What's for lunch?"

So with my kids I talk about accommodations. I talk about accessibility. I talk about different people having different ways of managing things. I talk about solutions that are and are not possible. I talk about the things I can do more skillfully than some other people, and the things that I absolutely cannot do. And how everyone has things that they absolutely cannot do, and that those things are different for different people.

My kids have seen people interact with me as though I am very much "other." They have asked me why I don't say anything, and I tell them that they just don't know, they are doing their best and it's unkind to call people out on things in public spaces. "They don't know me yet. It's fine. Everyone needs to learn. I'm fine with them learning at whatever pace they learn at."

They know I tell people "my ears are broken, I use my eyes to hear, so just look at me when you talk." Because people respond well to that. It's always a crapshoot if I use the words "deaf" or "hearing impaired" because people have ideas about what that means. And they know that they shouldn't call anyone else's ears "broken."

This means that when my kids are confronted with "disability awareness" they aren't immediately able to identify me as a part of that group of "others."

And honestly, that is how disability awareness should be taught. When we are truly aware of what disability is, it is impossible to view people as "other." We all need accommodations.

Another way we other people with disabilities is when we categorize people as either "good" or "bad," based on their behavior. We assign malicious intent based on things we have been told about what behavior means about people. Lauren Melissa Ellzey explains autistic meltdown from her perspective, based on her lived experience as an autistic person, in an article on NeuroClastic, "Autism and Meltdowns: One Autistic Woman's Journey." She tells about a time when a peer surprised her with an opposing social justice stance that evoked strong feelings in her and that, combined with the effects of the demands that had been placed on her related to social expectations, pushed her into meltdown.

> Some might say that my actions were meant to force my friend into following my personal set of beliefs. But what was really going on? In my personal experience, I have never had a meltdown that was intended to control the actions of others.
>
> Bashing my head into walls, shrieking in psychache, and throwing objects have never been my method of conflict resolution. In fact, these extreme measures represent the physical manifestation of my inner turmoil. Somehow, somewhere along the way, my sensory, social, and personal needs had been swept under the rug. Under the pressure to be as neurotypical as possible, I buried my fears and frustrations until my stress levels combusted.

People who frequently struggle with behavioral reactions to emotional dysregulation secondary to disability often find themselves othered, whether those doing the othering do it consciously or subconsciously.

What Does This Look Like in Action? Manifestations of Othering Disability

1. Using disability to get a laugh

An obvious manifestation of Othering Disability is when disability is used to get a laugh at the expense of a disabled person or group. This can range from jokes about disability to costumes that insensitively portray disability in an attempt to be funny.

In a blog post titled "Disability, Ableism, and Humour" on Medium, Ainslee Hooper tells about an incident that included making a joke about her own disability and her husband asking if it was ableist. She decided to dive into this question and the factors that go into determining when a joke is, and is not, ableist. She offered the following:

1. It's totally ok to laugh when a disabled person is making a joke about themself.
2. It's not ok to laugh at the expense of a disabled person. . . .
3. You're being ableist if you're a non-disabled person making a joke about disabled people.

A couple of years ago at Halloween, someone on my local Nextdoor group made a post asking if anyone knew the two blind kids who were out trick-or-treating because they were being destructive with their "sticks." I told the person that blindness was most likely their costume and that blind people don't typically walk around on Halloween, or any day, using their canes to try to damage property. I was very disheartened, similar to how I felt in 2017 when the Internet was laughing about the pilot who put on sunglasses and walked around the airport with a cane to make people laugh. Disability is not a punchline.

Challenge Yourself

Make sure the jokes you tell and share are not at the expense of disabled people. If you are in the presence of a nondisabled person who makes a joke about disability, call it out or, at the very least, don't laugh. If you are making plans for a costume that is going to make everyone laugh, take anything related to disability off the table.

If your child is ever witness to an offensive disability joke, make sure to take the time to explain why it isn't funny. Simply not laughing or getting quiet might leave your child with questions as they try to understand why some people seem to find it funny while others don't. Having a conversation about when jokes go too far can be impactful when your kids reach the age of understanding. I have explained it to my kids like this: if someone tells a joke about another person or group, but that person or group doesn't think it's funny, then it's not appropriate.

2. Perpetuating ableism through disability awareness campaigns

This one might sting, so remember that shame has no place here and that learning sometimes comes with discomfort. I fully realize that this way of othering comes from good intentions. Designating days, weeks, and months to awareness of specific disabilities *can* be a way that othering manifests. I bring this to the table because it is sometimes during these awareness activities and outreach that blatant examples of ableism show up.

Since we have already learned about many forms of ableism in this book, I'm going to take this opportunity to do an applied learning exercise. Let's say it's the first day of Blindness Awareness Month and a blind student's school community has decided to make the day all about blindness. The blind student shows up to school that day and is met with a barrage of staff telling him how he is their hero. Peers approach him to ask specific questions about his visual impairment. Are your alarm bells from chapter 2 and chapter 11 going off? A flyer about blindness is distributed, and a peer asks him if he will ever get his vision back. Another says he gets around so well that it's hard to tell that he is blind. The blind student is bombarded with multiple forms of ableism throughout the day, but no part of the disability awareness day is spent on talking about ableism.

Can you imagine how a situation like this might feel to the disabled person? It's true that awareness campaigns can be a way to educate and often strive to make disabled people feel seen, but they also create an "othering" dynamic. When the population incidence of a condition is low enough that there is a perceived need for an awareness campaign, that means very few individuals will likely be singled out. That individual or those individuals will essentially be in a category all their own and will have a great deal of attention focused on them, whether they like it or not.

My intention by including awareness campaigns is not to make you feel shame for activities and events you have participated in but, rather, to empower you with considerations that you can use in the future. If you are tasked with running a disability awareness event, or are considering participating in one, keep in mind all that you have learned here. As a result, you can show up as someone who will be better informed to participate in ways that are not perpetuating ableism when it is clear that your intention is to be supportive.

Challenge Yourself

If participating in awareness events, with or without your kids, be very mindful of the ways that disability is being represented, and for what reasons. If there is a fundraising component, try to find out where the money will go. There are many disability-related organizations, but not all are ethical or supported by people with the disability in focus. Pay attention to the way the event is being promoted and what is being stirred in people. If the event or campaign attempts to stir shock or pity, implies tragedy, or infantilizes, it is operating on ableism and, therefore, further perpetuating it. Depending on your relation to the campaign and personal relationships, you can decide whether to try to participate, educate, or pass.

If involving your kids in awareness activities or campaigns, be mindful of how you explain why participating is important. Avoid messages that include ableism. Thinking ahead about how I will explain something to my kids is often a personal litmus test to determine if what I'm doing is the right thing to do.

"We are going to an event today to support National Mobility Awareness Month because the money raised is going to be used to build an accessible playground in our community. Accessibility is really important for everyone." Consider the impact of that kind of framing versus something like "We're going to an event today to support National Mobility Awareness Month because it's so sad that some kids have to use wheelchairs and the money raised will pay for a playground that kids in wheelchairs can use."

I love the idea of teachers doing an access and accommodation inventory for all kids in their classroom at the beginning of every year, so that students with disabilities don't need to be singled out and thus othered because of their differences. If at the beginning of the school year every child is asked questions like "How do you best access written words?" and it is explained that some students access written words with their eyes, some with braille, and some through listening to the words read aloud, there is room for variety without making the child with the disability the only one discussing access.

A resource called "Whole Body Listening," available on Everyday Regulation's website and social media accounts, aims to do something similar but is specifically related to listening/attending. It comes in a

format that can be filled out by individual students and includes questions like "My eyes help me listen when . . ." and "My hands help me
listen when they . . ." Resources like this address accommodations by
allowing each student the freedom to do what his or her body needs to
do to learn. Some children use their eyes to help them listen by looking
at the teacher, while other children prefer not looking at the teacher
because eye contact is uncomfortable or distracting. More efforts to
recognize and embrace individuality will naturally reduce othering.

3. Treating disability like a spectacle

Behaviors like staring, pointing, talking about a person without their
participation, and responding to their presence with a sense of wonder, astonishment, disgust, or bewilderment are all examples of this
manifestation of othering. I understand wonder and curiosity when
something is novel, but when another human is involved, we must be
mindful of our actions and the way they make people feel.

Challenge Yourself

Recognize that disability is a normal part of the human condition
and refrain from treating disabled people differently. Consider how
you would feel if being treated this way, for any reason. People know
that their intentions are good and often assume that the person being
gawked at will receive the gawking with their non-ill intentions. Most
people aren't comfortable being gawked at, though. If you find yourself
doing this, ask yourself if you are treating the disabled person the same
way that you would treat an animal at the zoo or exhibit at a museum.

   If your child reacts in this way, there isn't any benefit to sham-
ing them for it, but it is important to talk to them about how being
treated that way might make the person feel. You can acknowledge
that they might never have seen someone with that kind of disability
before and that curiosity is natural. It is important, however, to go on

to explain there are certain ways to be curious that do and don't feel good to others. In the moment, consider something like "I know that you are wondering about that person, but shift your eyes to me for second so I can tell you a few things." If you handle these situations discreetly, you might redirect the staring before the disabled person has noticed and intercept othering. Even if the disabled person does notice, handling it with subtlety means it won't turn into a scene. When parents scold their kids for staring, it draws attention not only to them but also to the disabled person, as people nearby naturally piece together what is happening. Beyond that, it can unnecessarily create negative associations with disability.

4. Lumping disabled populations together

When it comes to groups that have been deemed to be different, lumping can present in a number of ways. In chapter 7, I referenced the lumping of perceptions and opinions of disabled people. This version of lumping happens when a disabled person is perpetually tied to the experiences of others with that same disability, by strangers.

In *Have Dog, Will Travel*, a blind guide dog student explains how this can look.

> The stranger once knew a blind guy in college, or a blind person who lived down the street. Sometimes he'll ask if I actually know the aforementioned person because, after all, shouldn't all blind people know one another? You're swallowing the damn muffin and you think "What if I asked if he knows all businessmen who wear London Fog raincoats?" . . .
>
> He knew a blind guy who climbed a mountain. He knew a blind guy who went skydiving. Who caught more fish than the rest of them combined. . . . And you want to say, "I knew a short guy once. I knew a short guy who could reach

the peanut butter on a shelf with a special device called a stepladder. He was amazing."

In this example, which is commonly shared among disabled people, the student relays how strangers feel compelled to lump together all their knowledge of, and experience with, blindness and then share it with the person who shares that disability. This manifestation is most likely fueled by a combination of an effort to connect with the disabled person and the ableism in them that is suggesting the way they typically converse with people doesn't apply to disabled people. It is the perceived distance between them and the disabled person, the "otherness," that compels this: "You are so different from mc that your difference is all that I think we have to talk about, and I assume that the little that I know about your disability will resonate with you."

Challenge Yourself

Believe that the same variability regarding opinions, preferences, associations, beliefs, and relationships exists among disabled people and nondisabled people alike. Even within the same disability, a person's experiences depend on a wide variety of factors. Understand that each person is an individual, and don't make assumptions about what common threads a person may or may not share with other disabled people.

Regarding children, much of what has already been indicated will be helpful for this manifestation as well. If you are modeling the value that every person is an individual with individual needs, your children will be well positioned to avoid lumping.

5. Disregarding the intersection of disability with other marginalizing aspects

Othering of Disability is compounded by other facets of a person's individuality. Many disabled people who are also part of additional marginalized communities share the ways that the intersections of their disability with other aspects of their identity compound the societal harm they face. In December 2022, Tiffany Joseph, an autistic writer, activist, and parent who goes by Nigh.functioning.Autism on social media, shared the ways that being Black often creates disabled people's need to suppress, and mask, their disabilities. The interview is called "Interview with an Autistic Adult" and was done by Chris Ulmer from the organization Special Books by Special Kids (SBSK). It can be found on SBSK's YouTube channel.

> CHRIS: I've noticed that a lot of the autistic advocates on social media happen to be White. Do they ever share things that might actually be counterproductive to the Black autistic community?
>
> TIFFANY: Yes. Unfortunately, it is, . . . I don't want to say mostly the case but, like, right there around 50 percent at least. Yeah. Because of the bias that others have for Black people, masking to just look hopefully as non-threatening as possible is necessary, and we might have to teach our autistic children to mask, even at school.
>
> CHRIS: What are some behaviors you might encourage your children to mask just to keep them safe?
>
> TIFFANY: Like, maybe, stim quietly? You know? No sudden movements. If you cannot speak to the officer, they're gonna deem you noncompliant, but it's better than reaching for a device. Having a meltdown would be so dangerous for a person who is Black. They look like they're being violent and aggressive. Where we see a lot of, and I see videos all the time, of autistic people who are White. They don't have the same . . . they might look aggressive but they might look disabled, they might look autistic to the officer. So, we cannot be our

disabled selves in certain situations, like maybe, White autistic people might not even know that. We are masking because of race as well. They might be masking their autism but we're masking because of race and autism.

Tiffany goes on to discuss how pro-disability movements that advocate for allowing people to be accepted as openly disabled, much like I am doing in this book, do not take into consideration that being openly disabled puts some people at a higher risk of harm. It is important that we do not neglect this reality in our efforts to make a safer place for people living with disability. If we are outraged by the mistreatment of disabled White people but decide that disability isn't a considerable factor when disabled Black people are mistreated, we are creating an additional layer of othering that serves as a barrier to inclusion and equity for all.

Challenge Yourself

First of all, it is important to listen to the voices of people from multiply marginalized groups and believe them when they express their experiences. In specific reference to disability and what we as community members can do, I think that pushing for the acceptance of all people existing as openly disabled is very important. For this acceptance to be extended to all, however, time and energy will be required of all of us.

This commitment can be met through pursuing avenues similar to what I have asked you to pursue for growth in understanding ableism. Seek out information and experiences specific to, and by, BIPOC disabled people and pursue resources that will help you deconstruct your own racial biases. A few additional people I have learned a lot from on social media are Tiffany Hammond (Fidgets and Fries), Imani Barbarin, Ola Ojewumi, and Talila "TL" Lewis. As we get closer to embracing the idea that all disabled people should be able to safely exist just as they are, we must not discount how racism and xenophobia create additional barriers. To actualize this for everyone, we need to be willing to put in the work to break those barriers down—*all* of them.

6. Polarizing "good" and "bad"

Another way that Othering Disability shows up is when certain traits are polarized as "good" or "bad." This manifestation can apply to physical appearance, behavior, and even educational performance.

Disabilities and physical differences have been exploited in entertainment for a very long time. *The Hunchback of Notre Dame* is an 1831 novel that centers a disabled character whose appearance is "monstrous," and there have been numerous examples since. In many forms of entertainment, characters are often given facial differences to make them seem more villainous, evil, or terrifying.

Behavior is very often polarized, which has a significant impact on those for whom emotional and behavioral challenges are secondary to disability. Numerous disabilities and conditions cause difficulty in managing emotional responses, and people who struggle to control their behavior are often painted as "bad." As an example, people who have an overactive amygdala, which can be the result of anxiety, depression, PTSD (post-traumatic stress disorder), or C-PTSD (chronic post-traumatic stress disorder), can struggle with managing emotional reactions. In the children's book *Poppy and the Overactive Amygdala* by Holly and Eric Proven, the ins and outs of brain functioning, as it relates to many aspects of thought and behavior, is explained. The book also explains what can happen when someone has an overactive amygdala. Poppy, the main character who has this condition, explains that she experiences a chronic state of "fight or flight" and describes how that manifests:

"Things that signal DANGER! to my hyper-alert brain might not seem dangerous to other people . . . but for me, my oversensitive Amygdala can't tell the difference."

She goes on to explain how moments of stress cause blood flow to move out of the prefrontal cortex, which is responsible for cognitive ability, decision-making, and judgment, and into the amygdala. She explains that this puts her in a state of fight or flight and talks about how flight, for her, sometimes means running. She then goes on: "Instead of running, my brain might decide to fight instead. This can mean arguing, yelling, or even hitting if I feel threatened. I don't like it when I fight. It's even worse when I rage."

The book shares helpful tips for how to help during a rage and continues with:

> After a rage, blood flow to my Prefrontal Cortex will start to return. My ability to reason and rationalize slowly comes back. I feel guilty and embarrassed about losing control. . . . During this time, it is important for me to know that I am still loved and forgiven. I hate thinking that someone is mad at me.

When challenging behavior is a factor, it is also common for people to determine that bad parenting is at play. In Jonathan Kohlmeier's memoir, *Learning to Play the Game: My Journey Through Silence*, Jonathan talks about how most adults at his school assumed the worst about him, and his parents, before they understood the challenges that selective mutism* can cause.

---

* Selective mutism (SM) is a condition that involves a high level of anxiety that can affect a person's ability to speak and often extreme anxiety related to social situations. Though SM is the diagnostic term that most are familiar with, in recent years many people who live with SM have suggested that the term *situational mutism* would be more appropriate and reflective of the reality of the condition.

Eventually, [the elementary school gym teacher] stopped yelling at me, but I don't think she understood why she should stop. I think she just didn't want to lose her job. Many times, the principal and the school psychologist had to talk to her. She wasn't alone. Before anyone knew I had a problem, everyone at school treated me like I was a difficult kid whose parents didn't know how to discipline their child.

Human nature often prompts us to jump to conclusions that we decide are the simplest. When we don't know the full story, we fill in the details and judgment happens quickly. Deciding that a child is bad, or that his or her parents don't know what they are doing, is the easy conclusion we have been conditioned by society to jump to.

I won't reduce or downplay the complexities of challenging behavior. Some behaviors are scary to witness, and some behaviors cause harm. This is in no way suggesting that scary and/or harmful behavior should be overlooked. What I am suggesting, though, is that simplifying these kinds of behaviors to an explanation of "bad" is typically inaccurate and urges your children away from compassion.

When Pete was in first grade, he shared with me that a friend of his was choking him on the playground. He shared that he knows this classmate "gets really mad sometimes but is really nice when she isn't mad" and was worried that if he told a teacher, she might get in trouble. I told him that I am thankful that he sees the good in people and knows that his friend wouldn't be acting that way if she weren't having a hard time. I went on, however, to reinforce that he has a right to safety and that telling a teacher is appropriate, because this friend needs more help with learning how to manage her feelings and behavior. I helped him understand that his safety is important, that it is never wrong to protect himself, and that his teachers would know how to help. With my assistance, we notified school staff, who called both children in to talk about it. The outcome was that the friend took responsibility and stopped hurting him, and they were able to remain friends.

What would have happened if I had said, "What kind of a kid chokes someone else? You just stay away from her. She's a bad kid." Not only would I be putting distance between my son and this friend, but I also would be sowing seeds of fear and "othering." It would have been my son and me against her, a first-grade child who was struggling with emotional regulation. Instead, I tried to help him understand that the problem was something his friend needed help with and that a solution that aims to solve that problem would benefit both of them.

Challenge Yourself

When someone's behavior is scary, harmful, or dismissive of the feelings of those around them, it is often hard to know the source of the challenging behavior. Often we won't ever know the factors a person is dealing with; nonetheless, we still strive to make sense of the behavior. Instead of reducing complex aspects of a person's humanity to the summation of "bad person," consider this explanation:

That person is having a hard time.

I really want you to sit with this line for a minute. It probably feels like a drastic oversimplification, but stick with me. You don't have to know the details of what is going on with a person to know, as truth, that the person is having a hard time. People don't generally act in harmful and scary ways when they are healthy and regulated. I urge this way of looking at behavior because a lot of good people—kids and adults alike—sometimes have a hard time managing their emotions and, consequently, their behavior. Judgment generally doesn't contribute to a positive outcome for anyone; the one judging causes separation between humans and the one judged feels more isolated. When someone is struggling, do we really need to know why to offer compassion? Does compassion need to be earned, or can we just freely offer compassion on the basis of suffering?

Sharing this way of viewing challenging behavior with your children is not the same as telling them to accept poor treatment. You can teach your kids to have compassion while maintaining their own safety and boundaries. Offering compassion is not the same as excusal, and chances are you have already modeled this for them if you have ever comforted them after they made a mistake that they still had to take responsibility for. You should also talk to your kids about how compassion does not require forgiveness. I tell my kids that when someone hurts them, it is normal to feel not only unsafe around that person but also mad at them. All feelings are OK, and having compassion for the person having a hard time does not exclude any feelings related to harm that they caused.

You can teach kids to say things like "I am sorry you are upset, but I am going to tell the teacher if you keep talking to me like that" or "It is not OK for you to hurt me with your body! I am going to get help."

I realize that kids don't always have support or protection, and sometimes it is important to create distance between children for the sake of safety. I maintain, though, that steering your kids toward the conclusion that someone is "bad" won't yield a more positive result than steering them toward compassion. When encouraging a more compassionate evaluation, you are reinforcing the truth that we often don't know what is under the surface for a person and that a situation can be far more complex than we realize. Sometimes your kid might be the one offering compassion, and sometimes your kid might be the one who could use the compassion.

Another factor to consider is the discrepancy between expectations and ability, which is more common than it should be. Because of misdiagnosis and lack of resources, children are sometimes put in situations that are outside of what they are capable of managing and do not have the support they need to deal with what is expected of them. When these children externalize their emotional dysregulation, i.e., struggle out loud, they sometimes earn a reputation among their peers as being the "bad kids." If you teach your kids that there is no such thing as a "bad kid," only "kids who have a hard time," you will be teaching them to resist the urge to polarize others in ways that generally lead to separation. They can make the necessary choices to protect themself regardless of which conclusion they land on. If you feel compelled to further explore this way of thinking about, and responding to, challenging behavior, I strongly recommend the book *Good Inside* by Becky Kennedy. It is not about disability but is an incredible resource for parents.

Bring It Home

In the children's book *A Day with No Words* by Tiffany Hammond, we get a glimpse into the ways that the main character, a young autistic boy, processes, experiences, and participates in daily activities. There is insight regarding how different types of sensory stimuli affect him and information about how he uses a communication device to communicate. In one part of the book, the boy and his mom are at the park. The illustration shows two moms with their kids nearby who are woefully staring at the boy, who is happily stimming a short distance away.

> There are some kids at the park with their mamas nearby.
> The clouds are still gray because the sky has just cried.
> They all turn to look at me as I jump and flap.
> One mother sneers "That boy is handicapped."

Later in the book, after his mom regains her composure, she responds to the other moms:

> "My son does not speak but his ears work just fine.
> The words that you say go straight to his mind."

It is rare to find children's books that address ableism head-on the way that *A Day with No Words* does. I find it critical to be explicit about these common occurrences that we so often sweep under the rug. In addition to this powerful aspect, the book tells a story from the perspective of a very underrepresented population with breathtaking beauty and clarity.

In the book *Insignificant Events in the Life of a Cactus* by Dusti Bowling, the story is told from the perspective of Aven, who has limb differences. Aven talks about a humiliating experience of being othered at school, and the resulting feelings.

> The worst had been when Mr. Jeffries, my art teacher, had asked the class if someone would pair up with me to help me get my paints ready. I couldn't have felt more put on the spot than if he had asked me to tap dance while balancing the paints on my head. I told him I didn't need help and could get the paints ready myself.
>
> The whole class had watched me the entire time, trying to pretend they weren't watching, as I had collected my supplies and arranged them at my workspace. It took me at least twice as long as most people to do things like this, and yet I still managed to be the very first person in the room to have all my paints ready. I guess the other kids had been too busy observing. I tried not to let it get to me. I reminded myself throughout the day that curiosity was normal; I shouldn't let it bother me.

I'm certain that Aven's teacher thought he was being helpful to Aven by asking classmates to assist her, but in doing so, he othered her. Aven's circumstances would have been much improved if he had done nothing and allowed Aven to carry on just as the rest of the class was. Treating people with disabilities no differently than we treat anyone else will help us avoid othering.

15

"SORRY, BUT WE DON'T HAVE A RAMP"

ABLEISM IN SYSTEMS AND INSTITUTIONS

IN THE ARTICLE "I Am a Lifelong Wheelchair User and I Don't Feel Welcome in the Church," found on *National Catholic Reporter*, Erin Murphy writes about the ableism she has faced in her church.

> Imagine going to Mass and not being able to get into a church building. Imagine going to confession and not being able to get into the confessional. Imagine a priest telling you that you are a burden to your parents. Imagine not being able to get on to the altar to be a lector, altar server or eucharistic minister.

Systemic ableism creates relentless and impactful barriers for people with disabilities. Following are excerpts from the court briefs from *Tennessee v. Lane*, a US Supreme Court case from

November 12, 2003, found on the Kansas Council on Developmental Disabilities website in an article called "Kansas's Disability Rights History":

> After decades of study, Congress determined that persons with disabilities had suffered from a virulent history of official governmental discrimination, isolation, and segregation. Congress found, moreover, that such discrimination and segregation, like race and gender discrimination, have repercussions that have persisted over the years and that continue to be manifested in decision making by state and local officials across the span of governmental operations. That official discrimination results not just in the denial of the equal protection of the laws and equal access to governmental benefits, but also in the deprivation of fundamental rights, such as the rights of access to the courts, to vote, to substantive and procedural due process, to petition government officials, and to other protections of the First, Fourth, Fifth, Sixth, and Eighth Amendments.

In "Fighting Ableism Is About Much More than Attitudes and Awareness," Andrew Pulrang gives examples of inaccessibility in different forms, which include the following:

- *Physical inaccessibility*, e.g., narrow doorways, inaccessible restrooms, inaccessible voting options
- *Information inaccessibility*, e.g., product information and entertainment content; incomplete access to news and emergency alerts
- *Outdated disability policies*, e.g., policies that penalize disabled people from working, saving and marrying; policies that fundamentally support disability segregation in varying forms

- *Overpowered social supervision and law enforcement,* e.g., programs that strip autonomy from those who need support; disproportionate share of police interference and violence
- *Intersection of ableism and other forms of oppression,* e.g., negative effects of ableism added to racism, sexism, homophobia, transphobia; income inequality and religious intolerance for multiply marginalized communities
- *Lack of disabled people in positions of power and influence,* e.g., underrepresentation of disability in elected officials; lack of accessibility at campaign events

There are many examples of inaccessibility that I was completely unaware of before I started research for this book. Accessibility challenges related to hotel rooms, taxis and transit services, voting, online applications, technology to work remotely, and websites are just a few examples that have been mentioned in accounts by disabled people. A friend who uses a guide dog has endured many instances of ride service drivers arriving to pick her up and either denying her a ride because of her service dog or simply driving right past. These additional barriers create frustration and exhaustion for people with disabilities.

Disabled people make up 15 percent of the population, and if your spaces are without disabled people, it might be because they are inaccessible. In a video on the #WeThe15 website, a large group of disabled people from all over the world and from all walks of life take turns sharing insights and jokes that address ableism and support advocacy. Near the end of the video, they share the following message: "And only when you see us as one of you, wonderfully ordinary, wonderfully human, only then can we all break down these barriers that keep us apart."

What Does This Look Like in Action? Manifestations of Ableism in Systems and Institutions

1. Denying access to civic and community activities and information

Although federal law requires that the act of voting be accessible, disabled people still report instances of accessible voting systems not functioning properly. Additional barriers exist that compromise, or eliminate, some disabled people's ability to vote. Physical access to voting locations can be problematic for disabled people who don't have reliable transportation options. Many who rely on rideshare or paratransit services report challenges with reliability and have shared stories about not being able to get to a polling location to vote. In addition, when voting in person is the only option, those who are medically vulnerable often can't risk their health by spending time in a busy polling location.

When communities don't ensure access to important public safety information—like emergency alarm systems—disabled people are at a higher risk of danger. The article "Access to Emergency Alerts for People with Disabilities" on WGBH.org shares that although many alert systems, services, and products are developing a range of text and audio capabilities that have the potential to serve people with disabilities, their inconsistent use creates challenges. If emergency broadcasts are not captioned, those who are d/Deaf and hard of hearing may not be alerted.

Challenge Yourself

Consider using your power as a constituent to enact positive change for the disabled community, even if it won't affect you directly.

Contact your neighbors to ask about access to voting and emergency alert systems. The Nextdoor app is one way to reach neighbors. If those in the community report unaddressed or unsolved barriers, consider reaching out to elected officials to voice your concerns. If disabled people are the only ones advocating for these changes, they may not be prioritized.

2. Limited access to child care for children with disabilities

Systems that support children are not free of systemic ableism. One such barrier that affects quality of life for children with disabilities is access to supportive child care. It is often very difficult for parents of disabled children to find child care options for their children. If a child docs not qualify for home care but has unique or complex medical or social-emotional needs, often the child is not accepted into child care settings. It is also common for children with complex social-emotional and behavioral needs to get kicked out of child care programs if the staff is not equipped to understand and support the child. Training is often necessary to support the needs of children who don't fit the mold, and access to training depends on a variety of factors.

Challenge Yourself

Advocate for funding for early childhood and after-school programs and specifically mention programs that support children with disabilities. If in-home child care providers feel more equipped to support disabled children, they will be more likely to accept them, and so community education is another important resource that community members can rally behind. The more informed a community becomes about disability, the more equipped it will be to support its disabled members.

3. Delaying access and accommodation due to age

I think it is assumed that since children probably won't remember instances during which they were left unaccommodated or underserved, it doesn't matter, and that there is still plenty of time to do these things before they make a significant impact. I disagree. When a child is developing their identity, how supported they are will play into the development of their self-worth and self-esteem. If they receive the message "It isn't important if you can consistently participate," children either become passive in their exclusion or have to spend extra energy to find ways to be noticed and included. Both can have damaging effects.

Dan and I often talk about accessibility in the places where he spends time. One of his biggest disappointments has been when videos that are not accessible are shown at school. When audio descriptions aren't provided, and no one is willing or available to describe the visual aspects to him, he reports feeling not only bored but also disregarded. I think many probably think of it in terms of "Not everything is going to be for you," but when everyone else can participate in an activity but your ability to participate is deprioritized right in front of you, it can feel very disappointing.

In the award-winning documentary *Crip Camp*, Jim LeBrecht talks about the toll that inaccessibility took on him as a teenager, as compared to his experience at Camp Jened, a New York summer camp for people with disabilities.

> At camp, I was in a whole other world. My first girlfriend, and I'm popular—and I'm going back to this world in which it's hard to get around. Sometimes I would just, like, go home after high school and go to bed for a few hours, and just get away from the world. I had friends but I'm the person with a disability. I had to try to adapt. I had to fit into

this world that wasn't built for me. It never dawned on me that the world was ever gonna change.

Challenge Yourself

You might think that it isn't necessary to take any steps if there isn't currently a disabled child in your child's class or community, but their absence could be related to systemic ableism. Disabled adults, and parents of children with disabilities, are constantly searching for accessible and inclusive places and activities. Accessibility is often a prerequisite, and when people make it a priority, even without a specific child in mind, it is an example of allyship in action. Between word of mouth, parent chatter in online groups, and community partnerships, the places you prepare will start to feel safe for your disabled neighbors. Just as Kevin Costner's character created a safe place for baseball in an Iowa cornfield in the movie *Field of Dreams*, you can make safe places in your communities for people with disabilities to thrive. "If you build it, they will come." (If that reference went over your head, I apologize. But, as a child of the 1980s, I couldn't resist.)

If you commit to taking one actionable step toward combating ableism in your community, using whatever position, opportunity, or platform you have, you can be part of positive change. You will not only be positively altering the world your kids will grow up in but also be providing a model for your children that they will learn from. Because the specific roles of those reading this book will greatly vary, there isn't any way for me to give specific ideas that will apply to everyone. Instead, I'm sharing a few resources that might help you figure out how to get started.

The ADA National Network (https://adata.org/) offers a wealth of information about accessibility and allows for customization based on who is searching for information. The nonprofit organization

Accessible Community (https://accessiblecommunity.org/) gathers individuals and groups to work together toward more inclusive communities. Its website includes a variety of resources to explain and support accessibility.

If you see red flags of systemic ableism in your community, here are a few ideas of ways that you can advocate.

- Scheduling meetings with directors of child care centers and schools and community leaders to talk about inclusive practices.
- Show up to school board meetings to make sure that those who make decisions that affect all disabled children in public schools prioritize access and disability rights.
- Reach out to organizations that serve children to extend support for teaching and training opportunities for staff to learn more about ableism and supporting children with disabilities.
- Reach out to community education leaders in support of community-wide access to disability education provided by disabled speakers and educators when possible.

Bring It Home

In January 2023, Susan-Elizabeth Littlefield of CBS News Minnesota reported a story about a fifth-grade class at Glen Lake Elementary in Hopkins, Minnesota, who raised $300,000 to purchase accessible playground equipment for their school. Students from the class shared explanations like "It just didn't seem fair that some kids were just left out" and "They didn't look happy, and recess is about having fun." They took the initiative to raise their concerns to their teacher, Betsy Julian, and made a plan to raise the money. A Glen Lake student who uses a wheelchair shared, "The first time I set foot on this playground, I'm probably gonna start crying, from seeing the effort that all the school has made." It's disappointing that the playground has been inaccessible for who knows how long, but I find it so encouraging to

hear a story about children noticing ableism and taking such determined initiative to make it right. Thinking about these kids growing
into leaders who will shape their own communities gives me a lot
of hope.

> Sometimes when we're together, we get stopped in our tracks.
> Like when all the fun and flavors of ice cream are just
> one step out of reach.
> We notice when things are unfair and it helps us get
> creative.
> We make plans. We solve problems.

This excerpt is from the book *We Move Together* by Kelly Fritsch,
Anne McGuire, and Eduardo Trejos. The illustrations show a family
approaching an ice cream shop, which has a step but no ramp. The
woman in the family is a wheelchair user, and she and her family
members look dismayed. On the next page, you see the family members and other community members doing different jobs necessary to
plan and install a ramp. This book is lovely for many different reasons.
If we take the initiative to notice when things are inaccessible and do
what we can to try to improve accessibility, we will be teaching our
kids the importance of accessibility.

Teaching your kids about disability history is another way to
empower a deeper understanding of ableism by providing examples
of innovations that have helped to combat it. The book *Six Dots: A
Story of Young Louis Braille* by Jen Bryant tells of the life and contributions of Louis Braille, including the development of braille.

> When I was older, I went to school with the other village
> children. All day, as they wrote down words and numbers
> or read out loud from printed pages, I sat in the front row,
> listening and memorizing. "Do you have books for blind

children?" I asked again. "No, Louis," the teacher replied. "I'm sorry." But I didn't want people to feel sorry for me. I just wanted to read and write on my own, like everyone else.

Understanding that disability rights and pushes for accessibility have come from a lot of hard work by a lot of people is an important part of allyship.

I Leave You with This

I hope this book has provided you with information and resources that will be helpful as you process and deconstruct ableism. I also hope it has given you confidence in being a nonableist leader and teacher for the children in your care. I want to leave you with one last quote from a children's book that can be an inspiration to all of us, but especially our littles. From *You Are Revolutionary* by Cindy Wang Brandt:

> You want to make change when you see things aren't right.
> But you wonder if you're too little or too shy to fight.
> Don't listen to those voices! There's so much you can do.
> You can be part of a revolution, just by being you.

BOOKS FOR YOUR CHILD'S LIBRARY

———

Beaty, Andrea. *Aaron Slater, Illustrator.*

Bell, Cece. *El Deafo.*

Bell, Davina, and Allison Colpoys. *All the Ways to Be Smart.*

Bowling, Dusti. *Insignificant Events in the Life of a Cactus.*

Brandt, Cindy Wang. *You Are Revolutionary.*

Bryant, Jen. *Six Dots: A Story of Young Louis Braille.*

Buell, Dusty. *Island of the Mix-Ups.*

Burcaw, Shane. *Not So Different: What You Really Want to Ask About Having a Disability.*

Burnell, Cerrie. *I Am Not a Label: 34 Disabled Artists, Thinkers, Athletes and Activists from Past and Present.*

Cowen-Fletcher, Jane. *Mama Zooms.*

Domnick, Margaret. *Everybody Has Something.*

Fritsch, Kelly, Anne McGuire, and Eduardo Trejos. *We Move Together.*

Hammond, Tiffany. *A Day with No Words.*

Heyworth, Melanie. *Just Right for You: A Story About Autism.*

Hunt, Lynda Mullaly. *Fish in a Tree.*

Lakin, Patricia. *Dad and Me in the Morning.*

Landreth, Corey, Andrea Landreth, and Jefferson Knapp. *Drawn to Be You.*

Miller, Winter. *Not a Cat: a Memoir.*

Millman, Isaac. *Moses Goes to a Concert.*

Moss, Deborah M. *Lee, the Rabbit with Epilepsy.*

Napper, Kristine. *A Kids Book About Disabilities.*

Omeiza, Kala Allen. *Afrotistic.*

Palacio, R. J. *We're All Wonders.*

Paxton, Lionel. *Guide Dogs! A Kids Book About Guide & Assistance Dogs.*

Penfold, Alexandra, and Suzanne Kaufman. *All Are Welcome.*

Proven, Holly, and Eric Proven. *Poppy and the Overactive Amygdala.*

Reynolds, Jason. *As Brave as You.*

Schuh, Mari. *My Life with Blindness.*

Sotomayor, Sonya. *Just Ask.*

Stuve-Bodeen, Stephanie. *We'll Paint the Octopus Red.*

Thomas, Nelly. *Some Brains: A Book Celebrating Neurodiversity.*

Willems, Mo. *Can I Play, Too?*

BIBLIOGRAPHY

Books

Anderson, Christopher. *Every Waking Moment: The Journey to Take Back My Life from the Trauma and Stigma of Stuttering*. Alexandria, VA: Just Confront Press, 2022.

Ashburn, Meghan, and Jules Edwards. *I Will Die on This Hill: Autistic Adults, Autism Parents, and the Children Who Deserve a Better World*. Philadelphia: Jessica Kingsley Publishers, 2023.

Ballou, Emily Page, Sharon daVanport, and Morénike Giwa Onaiwu, eds. *Sincerely, Your Autistic Child: What People on the Autism Spectrum Wish Their Parents Knew About Growing Up, Acceptance, and Identity*. Boston: Beacon Press, 2021.

Burnett, Frances Hodgson. *The Secret Garden*. Philadelphia: J. B. Lippincott, 1911.

Findlay, Carly. *Say Hello: How I Became My Own Fangirl; A Memoir and Manifesto on Difference, Acceptance, Self-Love and Belief*. 4th Estate, 2019.

Henley, Ariel. *A Face for Picasso: Coming of Age with Crouzon Syndrome*. New York: Farrar, Straus and Giroux, 2021.

Heumann, Judy. *Being Heumann: An Unrepentant Memoir of a Disability Rights Activist*. Boston: Beacon Press, 2021.

Higashida, Naoki. *The Reason I Jump: The Inner Voice of a Thirteen-Year-Old Boy with Autism*. New York: Random House, 2016.

Hull, Eliza, ed. *We've Got This: Stories by Disabled Parents*. Collingwood, VIC: Black Inc., 2022.

Jones, Chloé Cooper. *Easy Beauty*. New York: Avid Reader Press, 2022.

Kennedy, Becky. *Good Inside: A Guide to Becoming the Parent You Want to Be*. New York: Harper Wave, 2022.

Kisor, Henry. *What's That Pig Outdoors? A Memoir of Deafness*. Champaign, IL: University of Illinois Press, 1990.

Kohlmeier, Jonathan. *Learning to Play the Game: My Journey Through Silence*. Lulu Publishing Services, 2016.

Kornfield, Jack. *Bringing Home the Dharma: Awakening Right Where You Are*. Boston: Shambhala, 2012.

Kuusisto, Stephen. *Have Dog, Will Travel: A Poet's Journey*. New York: Simon & Schuster, 2018.

Ladau, Emily. *Demystifying Disability: What to Know, What to Say, and How to Be an Ally*. California & New York: Ten Speed Press, 2021.

Mavir, Heidi. *Your Child Is Not Broken: Parent Your Neurodivergent Child Without Losing Your Marbles*. Authors and Co., 2023.

Pinto, Jo Elizabeth. *Daddy Won't Let Mom Drive the Car: True Tales of Parenting in the Dark*. Self-published, 2019.

Saks, Ellyn. *The Center Cannot Hold: My Journey Through Madness*. New York: Hachette, 2008.

Silberman, Steve. *NeuroTribes: The Legacy of Autism and the Future of Neurodiversity*. New York: Avery, 2016.

Silverman, Arielle. *Just Human: The Quest for Disability Wisdom, Respect, and Inclusion*. Disability Wisdom Publishing, 2021.

Taussig, Rebekah. *Sitting Pretty: The View from My Ordinary Resilient Disabled Body*. New York: Harper One, 2020.

Wong, Alice, ed. *Disability Visibility: First-Person Stories from The Twenty-First Century*. New York: Vintage, 2020.

———, ed. *Disability Visibility: 17 First-Person Stories for Today (Adapted for Young Adults)*. New York: Delacorte Press, 2021.

———. *Year of the Tiger: An Activist's Life*. New York: Vintage, 2022.

Videos/Non-textual Media

BBC Three. "Things People with Down Syndrome Are Tired of Hearing." Via YouTube, August 2, 2016. https://www.youtube.com/watch?v=AAPmGW-GDHA.

Burridge, Kate. "Euphemisms." TEDx, via YouTube, June 22, 2012. https://www.youtube.com/watch?v=tpCTgNyA3DY.

CoorDown. "Not Special Needs." Via YouTube, March 16, 2017. https://www.youtube.com/watch?v=kNMJaXuFuWQ.

Crip Camp. Directed by Nicole Newnham and Jim LeBrecht. Netflix, 2020.

Deer, Beth. "AM I Right? Don't Pet My Guide Dog." AMI: Accessible Media Inc., via YouTube, October 30, 2019. https://www.youtube.com/watch?v=ye89hxHGyFM.

den Houting, Jac. "Why Everything You Know About Autism Is Wrong." TEDx, via YouTube, November 1, 2019. https://www.youtube.com/watch?v=A1AUdaH-EPM.

ESPN.com. "Karen Ryan Passing on a Love of Sports to Her Daughter Violet." July 24, 2019. https://www.espn.com/video/clip?id=27246112.

Facing History & Ourselves. "How Stereotypes Affect Us and What We Can Do." Last updated February 14, 2014. https://www.facinghistory.org/resource-library/how-stereotypes-affect-us-what-we-can-do.

Hubbard, Gem "10 Reasons Why You Should Never Touch a Wheelchair (Without Asking)." Wheelsonheels, via YouTube, September 9, 2020. https://www.youtube.com/watch?v=HvdlSAWLAOg.

Jeremy the Dud. Directed by Ryan Chamley. Robot Army Productions, via YouTube, 2017. https://www.youtube.com/watch?v=qFcFpWzIQNk.

Kellgren-Fozard, Jessica. "Oops, You Did an Ableism." Via YouTube, February 12, 2021. https://www.youtube.com/watch?v=fyGeX8gqx58.

Lisi, Ethan. "What It's Really Like to Have Autism." TED, via YouTube, April 29, 2020. https://www.youtube.com/watch?v=y4vurv9usYA.

Littlefield, Susan-Elizabeth. "Some West Metro Kids Are on a Mission to Provide Fun for All." CBS News Minnesota, December 5, 2022. https://www.cbsnews.com/minnesota/news/some-west-metro-kids-are-on-a-mission-to-provide-fun-for-all/.

My Dad Matthew. Directed by John Schaffer. Wild Asparagus Productions, via YouTube, May 27, 2019. https://www.youtube.com/watch?v=EsVzlyD7ArM.

Open Stutter. "A Lesson in Vulnerability from a Speech Therapist Who Stutters." Via YouTube, May 25, 2022. https://www.youtube.com/watch?v=3xKQsksUlsA.

Raising Dion. Created for television by Carol Barbee, based on the comic book by Dennis Liu. Netflix, 2019–2022.

Reason I Jump, The. Directed by Jerry Rothwell, inspired by book by Naoki Higashida. Kino Lorber, 2020.

Rivera, Lyric. "Autistic and NeuroDivergent Masking, Unmasking, and Burnout." Via YouTube, September 14, 2022. https://www.youtube.com/watch?v=lnd8Ih2UGJ0.

Special Books by Special Kids. "An Interview with an Autistic Adult." Via YouTube, December 6, 2022. https://www.youtube.com/watch?v=OOa-HOuBTCQ.

#WeThe15. Official website. Accessed March 18, 2024. https://www.wethe15.org/.

Wright, R. J. "Dyslexia." Button Poetry, via YouTube, July 7, 2020. https://www.youtube.com/watch?v=TZcAumLR2KE.

Young, Stella. "I'm Not Your Inspiration, Thank You Very Much." TED, via YouTube, June 9, 2014. https://www.youtube.com/watch?v=8K9Gg164Bsw.

Podcasts

Accessible Stall, The, hosted by Emily Ladau and Kyle Khachadurian. Episode 101, "Being Disabled Is Kinda Like *The Truman Show*." March 11, 2022. https://podcasts.apple.com/us/podcast/101-being-disabled-is-kinda-like-the-truman-show/id1105184406?i=1000553725583.

ADHD for Smart Ass Women, hosted by Tracey Otsuka. Episode 201, "Traumatic Brain Injury, Multiple Sclerosis and ADHD with Amanda Smith." Via YouTube, November 9, 2022. https://www.youtube.com/watch?v=8UeopQJb1SE.

Autism & ADHD Diaries, hosted by Danielle Punter. "Understanding Functioning Labels, Masking and the Challenges They Cause." February 22, 2021. https://podcasts.apple.com/ph/podcast/understanding-functioning-labels-masking-and/id1553532583?i=1000510156412.

Crutches and Spice, hosted by Imani Barbarin. "#CantMarryMyLove with Tito Quevedo." December 7, 2019. https://crutchesandspice.com/2019/12/07/cantmarrymylove-with-tito-quevedo/.

Stuttering Foundation Podcast, hosted by Sara MacIntyre. "Every Waking Moment with Christopher Anderson." November 9, 2022. https://www.stutteringhelp.org/podcast/every-waking-moment-christopher-anderson.

That Voice Podcast, hosted by Sally Prosser. Episode 74, "Changing the Stuttering Story with Marc Winski." April 18, 2021. https://podcasts.apple

.com/au/podcast/74-changing-the-stuttering-story-with-marc-winski /id1475068489?i=1000576843969.

Two Hot Takes, hosted by Morgan Absher. "Disabled NOT Differently Abled Ft. Molly Burke." Via YouTube, September 15, 2022. https://www.youtube .com/watch?v=zXA60rgL4lA.

Social Media Pages

Anner, Zach. Facebook. https://www.facebook.com/zachannerfanpage/.

Barbarin, Imani. Crutches and Spice. Instagram. https://www.instagram.com /crutches_and_spice/.

Bolton, Dannii. PDA Our Way. Instagram. https://www.instagram.com/pda_our_way/.

Burcaw, Shane and Hannah. Squirmy and Grubs. Facebook. https://www .facebook.com/squirmyandgrubs/.

Dacy, Alex. Wheelchair Rapunzel. Facebook. https://www.facebook.com/wheel chairrapunzel/.

Disabled in Massachusetts. Facebook. https://www.facebook.com/KbSmiless/.

Everyday Regulation. Facebook. https://www.facebook.com/everydayregulation/.

Ferraro, Anthony S. Facebook. https://www.facebook.com/asfvision/.

Findlay, Carly, OAM. Instagram. https://www.instagram.com/carlyfindlay/.

Forbes, Kristy. Autism & ND Support. Facebook. https://www.facebook.com /inTunePathways/.

Hahn, Carrie Cherney. iNFORM. Facebook. https://www.facebook.com/inform speechandlanguage/.

Hammond, Tiffany. Fidgets and Fries. Instagram. https://www.instagram.com /fidgets.and.fries/.

Hayden, Chloé. Facebook. https://www.facebook.com/chloeshayden.

Hazelwood, Rachel. Hazelwood Consulting. Facebook. https://www.facebook .com/hazelwoodconsulting/.

Joseph, Tiffany. Nigh.functioning.Autism. Instagram. https://www.instagram .com/nigh.functioning.autism.

Lewis, Talila "TL." Instagram. https://www.instagram.com/talilalewis/.

Life Through My Lens. Facebook. https://www.facebook.com/lifethroughmylens20/.

NeuroWild. Facebook. https://www.facebook.com/p/NeuroWild-100087870753308/.

Nurshable. Facebook. https://www.facebook.com/Nurshable/.

Ojewumi, Ola. Instagram. https://www.instagram.com/olas_truth/.

Open Future Learning. Facebook. https://www.facebook.com/OpenFutureLearn ingOfficial/.

PAST—Positive Assessments Support and Training. Facebook. https://www .facebook.com/LauraKerbeyPast.

Rivera, Lyric. Neurodivergent Rebel. Facebook. https://www.facebook.com/Neuro divergentRebel/.

Special Books by Special Kids (SBSK). Facebook. https://www.facebook.com /specialbooksbyspecialkids/.

Uncle Tics. Facebook. https://www.facebook.com/uncletics/.

Wilson, Jess. Diary of a Mom. Facebook. https://www.facebook.com/adiaryofamom/.

Online Articles

Aparna R. "The Burden and Consequences of Self-Advocacy for Disabled BIPOC." Disability Visibility Project, July 19, 2020. https://disabilityvisibility project.com/2020/07/19/the-burden-and-consequences-of-self-advocacy -for-disabled-bipoc/.

Bailin, Aiyana. "What the Fidget Spinners Fad Reveals About Disability Discrimi- nation." Thinking Person's Guide to Autism, May 20, 2017. https://thinking autismguide.com/2017/05/what-fidget-spinners-fad-reveals-about.html.

Barnes, Stephanie. "Suffering in Silence: The Epidemic of Invisible Disabilities in the Workplace." Medium, September 15, 2020. https://medium.com/swlh /suffering-in-silence-the-epidemic-of-invisible-disabilities-in-the-workplace -8ae2cc7eee86.

Belfield-Martin, Leenika. "Hey, Your 'Black Friend' Here—Stop Using Me." Pop- Sugar, August 28, 2020. https://www.popsugar.com/smart-living/having-black -friends-doesn't-make-you-anti-racist-essay-47533208.

Block, Laurie. "Stereotypes About People with Disabilities." Disability History Museum, accessed January 27, 2024. https://www.disabilitymuseum.org/dhm /edu/essay.html?id=24.

Blume, Harvey. "Neurodiversity: On the Neurological Underpinnings of Geekdom." Atlantic, September 1998. https://www.theatlantic.com/magazine/archive /1998/09/neurodiversity/305909/.

Burgmann, Jennifer. "What Independence Means to Me as a Person with a Dis- ability." The Mighty, June 18, 2019. https://themighty.com/topic/disability /disability-defining-independence/.

Butts, Amber. "This 'Raising Dion' Story-Line Is a Powerful Lesson on Consent, Disability and Possession." *RaceBaiter*, December 11, 2019. https://racebaitr .com/2019/12/11/this-raising-dion-story-line-is-a-powerful-lesson-on-consent -disability-and-possession/.

Catherine S. "How to Avoid 'Inspiration Porn' When Talking about Disability." The Mighty, July 2016. https://themighty.com/2016/08/how-to-avoid-inspiration -porn-when-talking-about-disability/ (page discontinued).

Clapton, Jayne, and Jennifer Fitzgerald. "The History of Disability: A History of 'Otherness.'" *New Renaissance* 7, no. 1 (1997). http://www.ru.org/index.php /human-rights/315-the-history-of-disability-a-history-of-otherness.

crippledscholar (blog). "Euphemisms for Disability Are Infantilizing." November 12, 2017. https://crippledscholar.com/2017/11/12/euphemisms-for-disability -are-infantalizing/.

Dominauskaitė, Jurgita, and Monika Pašukonytė. "6YO with Special Needs Has Tent Nobody Can Enter as Her Safe Space, Guests Are Upset That It Was Put Up in the Living Room." Bored Panda, January 5, 2023. https://www.bored panda.com/tent-toys-nieces-nephews-not-allowed-use/.

Doren, B., J. Gau, and L. Lindstrom. "The Relationship Between Parent Expectations and Postschool Outcomes of Adolescents with Disabilities." *Exceptional Children* 79, no. 1 (October 2012): 7–23. https://doi.org/10.1177/001440291207900101.

Douglas, Kelly. "How Ableism Affects the Mental Health of Disabled People." The Mighty, May 30, 2021. https://themighty.com/topic/disability/how-ableism -affects-mental-health-disability/.

Doyle, Nancy. "Is Everyone a Little Autistic?" *Forbes*, January 16, 2021. https://www .forbes.com/sites/drnancydoyle/2021/01/16/is-everyone-a-little-autistic/.

Ellison, Brooke. "Injustice Anywhere: The Need to Decouple Disability and Pro-ductivity." Petrie-Flom Center, Harvard Law, March 22, 2022. https://blog .petrieflom.law.harvard.edu/2022/03/22/injustice-anywhere-the-need-to -decouple-disability-and-productivity/.

Ellzey, Lauren Melissa. "Autism and Meltdowns: One Autistic Woman's Jour-ney." NeuroClastic, November 2, 2020. https://neuroclastic.com/autism-and -meltdowns-one-autistic-womans-journey.

endever*. "We Deserve Access to AAC." *homo qui vixit* (blog), January 2, 2019. https://anotherqueerautistic.wordpress.com/2019/01/02/we-deserve-access -to-aac/.

Farinas, Creigh. "Don't Call My Sister 'Cute': 6 Good Reasons to Stop Infantilizing Disabled People." Everyday Feminism, December 5, 2015. https://everyday feminism.com/2015/12/infantalizing-disabled-people/.

Fontenot, Stephen. "Study Challenges Assumptions About Social Interaction Difficulties in Autism." University of Texas at Dallas News Center, January 27, 2020. https://news.utdallas.edu/health-medicine/autism-social-interactions-2020/.

Gimeno, Jessica. "Stop Asking Disabled People 'What Happened to You?'" Fashionably Ill, December 6, 2018. https://jessicagimeno.com/stop-asking-disabled -people-what-happened-to-you/.

Hooper, Ainslee. "Disability, Ableism and Humour." Medium, January 6, 2022. https://ainsleehooperconsulting.medium.com/disability-ableism-and -humour-3c5a1a89b896.

Johnson, Rachelle. "Forming a Disability Identity as a Dyslexic." Office of Special Education and Rehabilitative Services Blog, October 19, 2021. https://sites .ed.gov/osers/2021/10/forming-a-disability-identity-as-a-dyslexic/.

Jones, Chuck. "Why No One Will Hire Me." Washington Post, October 29, 2006. https://www.washingtonpost.com/archive/opinions/2006/10/29/why-no -one-will-hire-me/1c3e963c-cfc3-4f7a-b557-55ffcaffc498/.

Kansas Council on Developmental Disabilities. "Kansas's Disability Rights History." Accessed March 18, 2024. https://kcdd.org/the-council/103-general -content/252-kansas-s-disability-rights-history.

Leahy, Morgan. "Stop Sharing Those Feel-Good Cochlear Implant Videos." Medium, August 17, 2016. https://medium.com/the-establishment/stop-sharing -those-feel-good-cochlear-implant-videos-f4bf63860ec.

Levis, Sarah. "Inspiration Porn: Once You See it, You Can't Not See It." Medium, November 12, 2019. https://medium.com/@GirlWithTheCane/inspiration -porn-once-you-see-it-you-cant-not-see-it-56296cb2fd37.

Love That Max (blog). "The Paradox of Disability Inspiration and May I Admire You, Please?" February 6, 2014. https://www.lovethatmax.com/2014/02/the -paradox-of-special-needs.html.

Mahipaul, Susan, and Erika Katzman. "What Does It Mean to Be 'Productive'? A Conversation Between Disability Allies." Medium, September 23, 2020. https://medium.com/national-center-for-institutional-diversity/what-does -it-mean-to-be-productive-a-conversation-between-disability-allies -e1bf32976ca2.

Meagan. "The Cost of Disability: Or, Why We Can't Have Nice Things." *Where's Your Dog* (blog), February 6, 2016. https://wheresyourdog.com/2016/02/06 /the-cost-of-disability-or-why-we-cant-have-nice-things.

Moore, James. "The True Cost of Being Disabled Goes Far Beyond Just the Physical." *Independent*, July 25, 2014. https://www.independent.co.uk/voices /comment/the-true-cost-of-being-disabled-goes-far-beyond-just-the -physical-9628374.html.

Murphy, Erin. "I Am a Lifelong Wheelchair User and I Don't Feel Welcome in the Church." *National Catholic Reporter*, April 5, 2021. https://www.ncronline .org/opinion/guest-voices/i-am-lifelong-wheelchair-user-and-i-dont-feel -welcome-church.

Murray-Nikkel, Allison. "Closed Captions and Neurodivergence." Empire Caption Solutions, December 29, 2021. https://empirecaptions.com/closed -captions-and-neurodivergence/.

Nović, Sara. "The Harmful Ableist Language You Unknowingly Use." BBC, April 5, 2021. https://www.bbc.com/worklife/article/20210330-the-harmful -ableist-language-you-unknowingly-use.

Parekh, Venessa. "Please Stop Calling My Life with a Disability 'Inspiring.'" Medium, April 8, 2016. https://medium.com/the-establishment/please-stop -calling-my-life-with-a-disability-inspiring-d8f6a6a27b72.

Parker, Melissa. "Disabled Women Like Victoria's Secret Model Sofia Jirau Don't Need You to Protect Them." *Unwritten*, February 28, 2022. https://www .theunwritten.co.uk/2022/02/28/disabled-women-like-victorias-secret-model -sofia-jirau-dont-need-you-to-protect-them/.

Perry, David. "How 'Inspiration Porn' Reporting Objectifies People with Disabilities." Medium, February 25, 2016. https://medium.com/the-establishment /how-inspiration-porn-reporting-objectifies-people-with-disabilities -db30023e3d2b.

Planning Across the Spectrum. "Here's Why You Should Stop Using Functioning Labels." August 18, 2020. https://planningacrossthespectrum.com/blog/why -stop-using-functioning-labels/ (site discontinued).

Pulrang, Andrew. "Fighting Ableism Is About Much More than Attitudes and Awareness." *Forbes*, June 14, 2021. https://www.forbes.com/sites/andrew pulrang/2021/06/14/fighting-ableism-is-about-much-more-than-attitudes -and-awareness/.

Romero, Daniel. "5 Things You Should Never Do to a Blind Person." *Thought Catalog*, April 2014. https://thoughtcatalog.com/daniel-romero/2014/04/5 -things-you-should-never-do-to-a-blind-person/.

See Jane. "2020 Film: Historic Gender Parity in Family Films." Geena Davis Institute on Gender in Media, 2020. https://seejane.org/research-informs -empowers/2020-film-historic-gender-parity-in-family-films/.

Shapiro, Matthew. "Disability Stereotypes That Won't Go Away." Inclusively, October 1, 2021. https://www.inclusively.com/matthew-shapiro-disability-stereo types-that-wont-go-away/.

Sibonney, Claire. "Americans Would Rather Be Dead than Disabled: Poll." Reuters, July 11, 2008. https://www.reuters.com/article/idUSN7B320259/.

Sinclair, Jim. "Don't Mourn for Us." *Our Voice* 1, no. 3 (1993). https://www.autism networkinternational.org/dont_mourn.html.

WGBH.org. "Access to Emergency Alerts for People with Disabilities." Accessed March 18, 2024. https://www.wgbh.org/foundation/services/ncam/access-to -emergency-alerts-for-people-with-disabilities.

Young, Stella. "The Wheel Perspective." Ramp Up, March 27, 2012. https://www .abc.net.au/rampup/articles/2012/03/27/3464847.htm.

INDEX

CHAPTER REFLECTION GUIDE

1. Do you have a personal connection to the form of ableism discussed in this chapter? Can you think of a time you witnessed, experienced, or perpetuated it?
2. What misunderstandings about this form of ableism were you operating from previously?
3. Which personal story or experience discussed in the chapter affected you the most?
4. What made that story or experience powerful or impactful for you?
5. Are there any passages that you would like to revisit later?
6. Is there any aspect of this form of ableism that you wish to learn more about?
7. Are there any personal changes you desire to make regarding this form of ableism?
8. How will you go about pursuing those changes?